May 2008

For Judy,

May you always find joy...

In Your Own Kitchen?

Reality Cooking at Home

♡ Karel Anne Tiessen

In Your Own Kitchen

Reality Cooking at Home

Copyright © 2008 by Karel Anne Tieszen

Book design by Soleil Design, Dallas, Texas

Primary Photos by Tracey Maurer Photography, San Antonio, Texas

Inset photos ©iStockphoto.com

Jacket photo of Chef by McCoys Photography, Duncanville, Texas

McCoy's Photography

All rights reserved. No part of this publication may be reproduced in any form by any means, electronic or mechanical, including photography and information storage and retrieval systems without permission in writing from the author.

Library of Congress Control Number: 2007942921

ISBN 9780977253203

Manufactured in the United States of America
First Printing 2008

WIMMER
COOKBOOKS

A CONSOLIDATED GRAPHICS COMPANY

800.548.2537 wimmerco.com

Table of Contents

Acknowledgements

There are many whose faith and support throughout my culinary adventures have encouraged my heart.

My original instructor, ***Tina Wasserman***, who gifted me two three-inch binders of recipes from the classes I attended. Her influence on my style and my life is clear, and I still publicly declare she is the best Jewish mother I never had.

Renie Steves, with whom I feel honored to share a profession.

A few well-known instructors who very directly informed me that I did not have enough culinary training and that my French was an embarrassment: I owe you a standing ovation because you strengthened my tenacity toward those goals.

Stephan Pyles, your trust and belief in me from the beginning has touched me more than you can imagine. Knowing you as a chef has been a culinary boon; knowing you as a friend has been a living blast!

Tracey Maurer, your photos brought tears to my eyes with their beauty.

Sheri Hall, your creative style is evident on every page.

Robin Plotkin Krasner, thank you for making my words flow with a culinary twist.

Dodee Crockett, who strategically assisted in making my dream of a year in Paris happen. You continue to be the one I want to squeeze my hand in all of my life paths.

Aurelia Harrison, in memoriam, who let me sit on the kitchen counter while she taught me the original family recipes, and the life stories that accompany them.

Susan Kelly Roomberg, an Austin College sorority sister who let me overflow her home with food we couldn't eat because it was for the photo shoots.

Aaron and ***Ambra***, my 'culinary monsters', who consumed multiple varieties of the same recipe while I was testing; who shared many international restaurants; and who are both confident and proficient when it is their turn to prepare dinner.

Finally, I would like to thank the Cast of Thousands: ***John***, ***Susie*** and ***Theodore Thousand***.

Foreword

In January of 1988, while teaching cooking classes at Cuisine Concepts in Fort Worth, I was caught off guard by one of my students who began asking what seemed like an inordinate amount of questions. Not just simple questions like "what can I substitute?," or "can I freeze it?," but theoretical and technical questions like, "why wouldn't I use Gewürztraminer instead of Riesling in a particular fish sauce" or "how are the stamens of the crocus harvested for saffron?" After being bombarded with such questions for the entire 3 hour class, it became painfully obvious that Karel Anne was much more than one of the other "weekend kitchen warriors" that usually attended my classes. That evening marked the beginning of a long and mutually respectful gastronomic friendship.

I have watched Karel Anne develop over the years from a curious and interested cook into a dedicated, skilled culinarian and teacher. She has taken serious risks and made tremendous sacrifices to follow her dream. She gave up a lucrative executive position with a respected corporation to open her cooking school. When she wanted to learn more about French Cuisine, she picked up her young family and moved to Paris, where she spent several years developing and honing her technique and submerging herself in its very culture.

We first became better acquainted when she volunteered her culinary services for a national charitable event I helped found called "Taste of the Nation," a fundraiser for Share Our Strength, the country's largest private hunger-relief organization. She continued to show up in my various cooking classes and became more and more committed to "Taste of the Nation." Eventually, after about six years of participating as a culinary volunteer, I asked her to be on the event committee. If memory serves, at the first meeting of that year, we were informed that our chairman was being transferred out of town with her job. When Karel Anne left for a bathroom break, the rest of the committee recommended that she replace the "relocated" chairperson. Upon her return, and much to her surprise, we congratulated her on her new "appointment" as chairperson for one of Dallas's most prominent charitable fundraisers. She (and the event) were a smashing success.

I have come to realize that Karel Anne has the capacity to do anything she really puts her (strong-willed) mind to. It's been her dream to publish a cookbook with the many recipes she's developed over the years. And here it is! I personally am so proud of her first efforts. The book basically follows the philosophies and themes of her cooking classes. It will not only appeal to people who cook regularly and frugally, however, but also to people who enjoy a creative "spin" on tried and true classics. Her "vignettes from life in a Paris kitchen" add a delicious element that is rarely seen in book of such good but simple virtues.

*As I open my new restaurant with its "state-of-the-art" cooking school, I already know who I want to teach as soon as a certain (*In Your Own Kitchen*) cookbook is published. I can only hope one of the curious students drills her on the production of saffron.*

—Stephan Pyles

Chocoholic Bread
Awaken to Apricot Blintzes
Tender Oatmeal Raisin Scones

Beginning With Breakfast

These taste like big, soft oatmeal cookies.

Tender Oatmeal Raisin Scones

1 1/2	cups all-purpose flour
1 1/2	cups old-fashioned rolled oats
1/3	cup brown sugar, packed – (light or dark)
1	Tablespoon baking powder
1	teaspoon salt
1/2	cup unsalted butter – cut up (1 stick)
1 1/2	cups raisins, seedless – (about 8 ounces)
1	cup milk
1	Tablespoon milk – (for brushing)
1	Tablespoon sugar
1	teaspoon cinnamon

1. Preheat oven to 425F.
2. Combine the flour, oatmeal, sugar, baking powder, and salt in a food processor. Pulse to combine. Add butter and pulse until the mixture resembles coarse corn meal.
3. Place mixture into a bowl, and mix in raisins. Add the milk, and stir well to combine.
4. Turn dough out onto a heavily floured (up to 1/4 cup) work surface. Fold over until dough holds together and is less sticky.
5. Divide the dough into three equal sections. Make each into a 5 inch round disk. Place on baking sheet. Using a floured knife or pastry scraper, cut the disks into 6 wedges.
6. Brush the tops of the scones with milk. Sprinkle with the cinnamon and sugar mixture. Bake for 18 minutes or until they are golden and firm.

For crispier (traditional) scones, use 2 cups of flour and 1 1/2 cups of quick cooking oats.

Makes 18 servings.
Per Serving: 173 Calories; 6g Fat (31.1% calories from fat); 3g Protein; 28g Carbohydrate; 2g Dietary Fiber; 16mg Cholesterol; 211mg Sodium.

As a timesaver, I find it helpful to put the uncovered dish into a cold oven. Let it preheat and bake for almost an hour while everybody gets ready in the morning.

Topple Over Peach French Toast

1/2	cup unsalted butter — (1 stick)
1 1/3	cups brown sugar, packed
29	ounces canned peaches — sliced, juice reserved
10	slices whole grain bread — cut in quarters
6	eggs — beaten
1 1/2	cups milk
1	Tablespoon vanilla

1. In a medium saucepan, melt butter. Stir in the brown sugar and juice from the peaches. Simmer until the mixture coats the back of a spoon. Pour into a greased 13 inch x 9 inch baking dish.
2. Place peaches in one layer over the sauce.
3. Tightly place the bread slices over the peaches, filling all gaps.
4. Beat the eggs in a medium bowl. Add milk and vanilla. Whisk briefly until a frothy foam appears. Pour over the bread, moistening each piece. Cover with plastic wrap and refrigerate overnight.
5. In the morning, preheat the oven to 350F. Remove plastic wrap and bake for 40 minutes.
6. Remove from the oven and allow to cool for up to 10 minutes. Place serving tray over the pan and invert. Serve warm.

Makes 12 servings.
Per Serving: 334 Calories; 13g Fat (33.2% calories from fat); 8g Protein; 49g Carbohydrate; 4g Dietary Fiber; 131mg Cholesterol; 245mg Sodium.

Saturday morning sleepy heads can't resist the smell of warm cinnamon

Overnight Cinnamon Rolls

- 2 packages active dry yeast
- 7 1/4 cups all-purpose flour
- 1/3 cup brown sugar, packed
- 2 teaspoons salt
- 1/2 cup water – hot
- 2 cups milk – lukewarm
- 1 egg
- 1/3 cup shortening
- 1/4 cup unsalted butter – softened, (1/2 stick)
- 1/2 cup sugar
- 2 Tablespoons cinnamon
- 1 cup powdered sugar
- 1 Tablespoon milk
- 1/3 cup sour cream

1. Blend the yeast, 7 cups flour, brown sugar, and salt with a fork in a large mixing bowl.
2. Pour the hot water and warm milk into the flour mixture and blend. As it incorporates, add the egg and shortening. Mix until smooth. Add up to 1/4 cup flour until the dough no longer sticks to the bowl.
3. Remove dough to a floured surface. Divide into two pieces. Using a rolling pin, shape each piece into a large rectangle. Brush the surface with butter.
4. Combine the sugar with the cinnamon and sprinkle over the dough. Roll each rectangle tightly, and cut each into 12 equal slices. Place on a greased baking sheet, cover lightly with plastic wrap and refrigerate overnight.
5. In the morning, preheat oven to 375F. Remove plastic wrap and bake for 20 minutes.
6. In a small bowl, drizzle the milk over the powdered sugar and stir to combine. The mixture will be very stiff. Add the sour cream and stir until smooth.
7. When the rolls come out of the oven, place them on a serving tray. Spread the sour cream frosting on top while they are still warm.

If adding raisins, use about 1/2 cup per rectangle and distribute evenly

What now?
Did the rolls rise excessively over the edge of the pan? Spray another pan with non-stick spray. Move three or four of the rolls to the new pan for plump rising and proper baking.

Makes 12 servings.
Per Serving: 477 Calories; 13g Fat (25.3% calories from fat); 10g Protein; 79g Carbohydrate; 3g Dietary Fiber; 37mg Cholesterol; 391mg Sodium.

Blue Berry Brights

1	pint blueberries
2	Tablespoons whole wheat flour
1 1/2	cups all-purpose flour
1/2	cup whole wheat flour
1/2	cup sugar
2	teaspoons baking powder
1/2	teaspoon salt
2	eggs – beaten
2	Tablespoons vegetable oil
1/4	cup unsalted butter – melted and cooled, (1/2 stick)
3/4	cup buttermilk

1. Rinse and pick through blueberries. Toss with the 2 Tablespoons of wheat flour. Set aside. Preheat oven to 375F.
2. Mix flours, sugar, baking powder, and salt in a large bowl with a fork. Aerate the flour and distribute the baking powder evenly for a rounded muffin.
3. Break eggs into small bowl. Drizzle oil into eggs while beating with a whisk. Drizzle cooled butter into the egg mixture in the same way. Add the buttermilk last, and mix until completely blended.
4. Using a spatula, create a well in the center of the dry ingredients. Pour wet ingredient mixture into the well, and mix quickly, but gently. Remember, the batter will be thick, and somewhat lumpy.
5. Fold in the blueberries, trying not to crush them with the thick batter. Spoon into greased or paper-lined muffin tins.
6. Bake for 25 minutes.

A version of this recipe is also found in the Kid's Collection chapter for smaller chef hands.

Optional topping: 2/3 cup flour, 1/2 cup brown sugar, 1/4 cup unsalted butter. Mix together with a fork until crumbly. Sprinkle on muffins just before baking.

Makes 12 servings.
Per Serving: 197 Calories; 7g Fat (33.3% calories from fat); 4g Protein; 29g Carbohydrate; 2g Dietary Fiber; 46mg Cholesterol; 200mg Sodium.

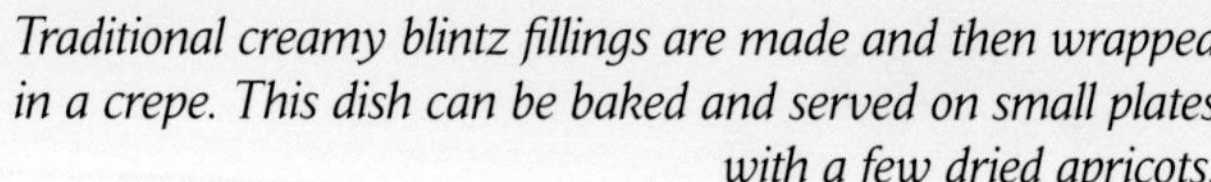

Traditional creamy blintz fillings are made and then wrapped in a crepe. This dish can be baked and served on small plates with a few dried apricots.

Awaken to Apricot Blintzes

16 ounces cottage cheese – small curd
18 ounces cream cheese – softened
2 egg yolks
1 Tablespoon sugar
1 teaspoon vanilla extract

1 1/2 cups sour cream
3/4 cup apricot preserves
2 Tablespoons orange juice
6 eggs
1/4 cup unsalted butter – softened, (1/2 stick)
2 cups flour
1/3 cup sugar
2 teaspoons baking powder
1/2 teaspoon cinnamon
2 Tablespoons powdered sugar

Low fat versions of cottage cheese (drained), cream cheese and sour cream work well in this recipe.

1. In a small bowl, beat cottage cheese, cream cheese, egg yolks, sugar, and vanilla until well blended. Set aside.
2. In a blender, combine sour cream, apricot preserves, orange juice, eggs, butter, flour, sugar, baking powder, and cinnamon. Cover and blend well, scraping sides occasionally. Pour half of the batter into a greased 13 inch x 9 inch pan.
3. Gently pour the cheese filling over the flour mixture. Spread evenly.
4. Pour remaining batter on top of filling. Cover, and refrigerate at least two hours, or overnight.
5. Bake in a preheated oven at 350F for 50–65 minutes or until puffed and light-golden brown. Serve hot. Top with powdered sugar, if desired.

Makes 16 servings.
Per Serving: 362 Calories; 22g Fat (53.6% calories from fat); 11g Protein; 31g Carbohydrate; 1g Dietary Fiber; 161mg Cholesterol; 316mg Sodium.

Glass Biscuits

2	cups all-purpose flour
2 1/2	teaspoons baking powder
1/4	teaspoon salt
1/2	teaspoon baking soda
1	Tablespoon sugar
1/3	cup unsalted butter – softened
3/4	cup buttermilk

1. Preheat oven to 375F.
2. In a large bowl, stir together flour, baking powder, salt, baking soda, and sugar with a fork.
3. Cut butter into chunks. Add to the bowl and rub mixture together with your fingertips until the largest pieces are no larger than 1/4 inch in diameter.
4. Pour in buttermilk. Stir until dough sticks together and clings to the fork in a large lump.
5. Remove dough from bowl onto a lightly floured surface. Turning the dough to coat all surfaces lightly with flour. Knead dough, turning over about ten times.
6. Place dough into a lightly greased 9 inch round cake pan. Pat dough out evenly to fill pan. With a flour dusted, 2 inch diameter drinking glass, cut straight down through the dough, then lift cutter straight up to make each biscuit, leaving everything in place in the pan. Cut close together to make as many as possible.
7. Bake in the oven for 15 to 20 minutes or until golden brown.

The odd shaped pieces usually go first at our house. We save the pretty ones for our guests, not letting on that the crescent shape holds both butter ***and*** *jam perfectly.*

If doubling the recipe, separate into two batches to knead. This avoids over-working the dough.

Makes 6 servings.
Per Serving: 263 Calories; 11g Fat (37.3% calories from fat); 5g Protein; 36g Carbohydrate; 1g Dietary Fiber; 29mg Cholesterol; 431mg Sodium.

"Can I have chocolate milk, too?"

Cocoa-Cuckoo Cinnamon Rolls

1	package yeast – quick-rising
2	cups all-purpose flour
1/3	cup cocoa
1/2	cup milk
1/4	cup water
1	egg
1/4	cup shortening
1/4	cup granulated sugar
1/2	teaspoon salt
2	Tablespoons butter – melted and cooled
1/4	cup granulated sugar
2	teaspoons cinnamon
1	cup powdered sugar
1	Tablespoon milk

1. Preheat oven to 375F.
2. Combine yeast, flour, and cocoa in a large mixing bowl. Combine milk and water in a microwave safe cup and heat until very warm to the touch, but do not allow to boil.
3. Turn mixer on low, and pour warm liquid into flour mixture. Add the egg, shortening, sugar and salt. Blend until smooth. Add tablespoons of flour as needed until the dough no longer sticks to the mixing bowl. Scrape dough into a greased bowl. Cover and allow to rise for 20–30 minutes in a warm place.
4. After rising, remove dough to a lightly floured surface. Using a rolling pin, shape into a large rectangle, about 12 inches x 9 inches. Brush with the melted butter. Sprinkle with the granulated sugar-cinnamon combination, and roll up.
5. Cut into 12 equal slices, and place on a greased cookie sheet. Allow to rise for 20 minutes, then place in the oven. Check the rolls after 20 minutes, and allow to bake an additional 5–10 minutes if required.
6. Combine powdered sugar and milk in a bowl, thinning with a few more drops of milk if desired. When rolls come from the oven, spread with frosting while still warm.

Makes 12 servings.
Per Serving: 223 Calories; 8g Fat (29.7% calories from fat); 4g Protein; 37g Carbohydrate; 2g Dietary Fiber; 24mg Cholesterol; 121mg Sodium.

This is based on a recipe from the bread table at our favorite all-inclusive resort.

Chocoholic Bread

1/2	cup all-purpose flour
1	package active dry yeast
1	cup warm water – 110 degrees
1	cup all-purpose flour
1	teaspoon vegetable oil
2 1/4	cups all-purpose flour
1	teaspoon salt
1	teaspoon vegetable oil
7	ounces chocolate – cut in large chunks

1. Mix 1/2 cup flour with the yeast in mixing bowl. Pour in water and mix quickly with a fork. Add remaining cup of flour and mix until it is a heavy paste (called a sponge). Cover with plastic wrap, and let the sponge rise until doubled.
2. Use 1 teaspoon oil to coat a large bowl for the second bread rising. Add 2 cups of flour, salt, and oil to the sponge and knead, or mix thoroughly with dough hook attachment. If the dough seems sticky, add flour, one tablespoon at a time, up to 1/4 cup. Wash hands in very cold water (or dip in ice water). Add chocolate and knead into bread using your fingertips to keep chocolate from melting. Scrape into the oiled bowl for rising.
3. Preheat oven to 450 degrees. When the oven reaches the desired temperature, place a cookie sheet on the lowest rack, underneath where the bread will bake. Add one cup of very hot water to the cookie sheet and quickly close the oven door.
4. Shape dough for the loaf, and place in pan, or on a baking sheet. Carefully check that no chocolate is directly touching the cookie sheet. (Burned chocolate aroma seeps into the rest of the good bread.) Place the pan on the middle rack of the oven. Add an additional 1/2 cup water to the lower cookie sheet. Bake for 15 minutes.
5. Remove the water cookie sheet and bake an additional 20 to 25 minutes. Bread should be a golden color. Remove from pan to cool on a rack. If left to cool on the sheet, the bottom will be steamed and soggy instead of a light crisp texture.
6. For best results, slice with a serrated knife.

Makes 18 servings.
Per Serving: 156 Calories; 5g Fat (25.5% calories from fat); 3g Protein; 27g Carbohydrate; 1g Dietary Fiber; 0mg Cholesterol; 121mg Sodium.

I like to use a pierced baguette pan so the bread can bathe in the steam and create the trademark French bread crust. A standard baguette pan is 15 inches long with two 3 inch wide cylinder compartments, and can be found in gourmet kitchen stores.

The optimum rising temperature for yeast is 80F. (Pretty easy in the kitchen on a summer Texas day!)

What now?
No baguette pan? Form loaves on a large cooling rack set over a baking sheet.

Just right to take tea with the Queen!

Sweet Barley Currant Scones

1/2	cup currants
3/4	cup water
1 1/2	cups barley flour
1	cup all-purpose flour
1	Tablespoon baking powder
1/2	teaspoon salt
1/2	cup unsalted butter – cut up (1 stick)
1/4	cup sugar
2/3	cup milk

1. Place currants in a glass dish or measuring cup, cover with water, and microwave for 30 seconds. Allow to stand while preparing other ingredients.
2. Preheat oven to 375F.
3. Put flours, baking powder, and salt in a food processor. Pulse to combine. Add the butter and sugar. Pulse until the mixture resembles ground corn meal.
4. Place mixture into a large bowl. Add drained currants and milk. Mix with a spatula until all ingredients are well blended.
5. Drop dough by tablespoonfuls onto an ungreased cookie sheet. Flatten with the spoon for an evenly baked scone. Bake for 15 minutes until pale golden brown.

From the preface of her NEW COOK BOOK, first published in 1902: "I have not compiled a recipe book, but have made a complete new book telling the things one needs to know about cooking, living, health, and the easiest and best way of housekeeping. Cookery puts into practice chemistry, biology, physiology, arithmetic, and establishes an artistic taste. And if our motto is, 'Let us live well, simply, economically, healthfully and artistically,' we have embraced all the arts and sciences."

—Sarah Tyson Rorer (1849-1937),
Culinary Editor of the **Ladies Home Journal** 1897-1911

Makes 15 servings.
Per Serving: 169 Calories; 7g Fat (35.4% calories from fat); 3g Protein; 25g Carbohydrate; 2g Dietary Fiber; 18mg Cholesterol; 176mg Sodium.

In an open market near Oslo, light thin pancakes like these are rolled into a napkin for a portable breakfast.

Norwegian Pancakes

1	cup whole wheat flour
1	cup all-purpose flour
1	Tablespoon sugar
2	teaspoons baking soda
1/8	teaspoon salt
1	egg
3	cups buttermilk
1/4	teaspoon vanilla extract

1. In a large bowl, combine flours, sugar, baking soda and salt, mix well with a fork.
2. In a medium bowl, beat the egg lightly with a fork. Add the buttermilk and vanilla and stir.
3. Lightly coat a nonstick griddle with cooking spray and heat over medium heat until a drop of water dances on it.
4. Make a well in the center of the dry ingredients. Pour in the buttermilk mixture and mix together just enough to moisten the dry ingredients.
5. Pour sufficient batter to make thin, 4 inch pancakes (you can fit about four on an 11 inch griddle). Cook until you can see bubbles in the batter. Flip them gently and cook on the other side until you see steam rising, then quickly remove them to a plate.
6. Spread pancakes with apple butter or fruit jam and roll up to eat with your hands. These can also be served as traditional pancakes with syrup and butter.

Makes 8 servings.
Per Serving: 161 Calories; 2g Fat (10.3% calories from fat); 7g Protein; 29g Carbohydrate; 2g Dietary Fiber; 30mg Cholesterol; 454mg Sodium.

Versatile for use with standard size and large Belgian waffle makers, too!

Light and Fluffy Waffles

- 3 eggs
- 2 cups buttermilk
- 1/4 cup butter – melted and cooled, (1/2 stick)
- 1/2 cup whole wheat flour
- 2 teaspoons baking powder
- 1 teaspoon baking soda
- 1/2 teaspoon salt
- 1 1/2 cups flour, all-purpose

1. In a large bowl, beat the eggs. Pour the buttermilk and the butter into the bowl and continue mixing until the eggs are incorporated. The mixture will look a little foamy.
2. Prepare the waffle iron with non-stick spray, then preheat.
3. In a small bowl, mix the wheat flour, baking powder, baking soda, and salt with a fork. (This keeps the powder and soda from staying in a lump in your mixture.) Add the all-purpose flour and the wheat flour mixture to the eggs. Stir until mixture is completely moistened.
4. Pour enough batter on the waffle iron to cover a little over half to two thirds of the griddle. Using a spoon, gently spread the mixture toward the edge, and close the waffle iron. In about 5 minutes, or when the steam stops rising, open the waffle iron and remove the waffle with a fork. Repeat with remaining batter. Serve hot.

Why mix the dry ingredients with a fork? This helps to aerate the flour and blend with the other ingredients. Your result is a much fluffier textured waffle.

For a clever dessert, try spooning fresh fruit over the waffles and adding a dash of powdered sugar.

Makes 8 servings.
Per Serving: 215 Calories; 9g Fat (35.7% calories from fat); 8g Protein; 27g Carbohydrate; 2g Dietary Fiber; 97mg Cholesterol; 562mg Sodium.

Overnight Oatmeal Raisin Pancakes

2 cups old-fashioned rolled oats
2 cups buttermilk
2 eggs
1/4 cup unsalted butter – melted (1/2 stick)
1/2 cup raisins, seedless
1/2 cup flour
2 Tablespoons sugar
1 teaspoon baking powder
1 teaspoon baking soda
1/2 teaspoon cinnamon
1/2 teaspoon salt

1. Mix oats and buttermilk in a large bowl. Cover and refrigerate overnight.
2. In the morning, beat eggs and butter in a small bowl. Stir raisins and egg mixture into oatmeal. Mix remaining ingredients, add to oat mixture and stir briskly, just until moistened. Let stand up to 20 minutes before cooking.
3. If batter seems too thick, add buttermilk one tablespoon at a time. Prepare the griddle with a non-stick spray. When griddle is hot, pour 4 inch pancakes without crowding. Cook pancakes until a few bubbles appear on the top, then turn to brown the other side. Watch the heat. If the griddle is too hot, the insides will be gummy and near raw.

Cinderella said to Snow White, "How does love get so off course? All I wanted was a white knight with a good heart, soft touch, fast horse."

—**This Kiss**
by Faith Hill

Makes 8 servings.
Per Serving: 314 Calories; 10g Fat (29.1% calories from fat); 11g Protein; 45g Carbohydrate; 5g Dietary Fiber; 71mg Cholesterol; 436mg Sodium.

Cranberries aren't just for winter holidays, you know.

Cranberry Scones

3/4	cup cranberries – rough chopped
1/3	cup sugar
1	teaspoon orange zest
3	cups all-purpose flour
1/4	cup sugar
4	teaspoons baking powder
1/2	teaspoon baking soda
1/2	teaspoon salt
1/2	cup unsalted butter – cut up (1 stick)
2/3	cup buttermilk
1	egg

1. Preheat oven to 375F.
2. In a small bowl, combine cranberries, sugar and zest. Set aside.
3. In a large bowl, combine flour, sugar, baking powder, baking soda, and salt. Using a pastry blender, cut in the butter until coarse crumbs form.
4. Make a well in the dry ingredients and stir in the buttermilk and egg just until moistened. Fold in the cranberry mixture.
5. If the dough is very sticky, sprinkle with flour. Turn dough onto a floured surface and knead just 5 or 6 times until the dough is well mixed.
6. Cut dough into 6 equal pieces, shape into balls and place on greased baking sheet. Bake 25 to 30 minutes until golden brown. Cut in half to serve.

Incorporating 1/2 cup finely chopped walnuts or pecans adds texture.

What now?
Couldn't resist the "Freeze One for Later" suggestion on the cranberry bag in the produce section? Well, you've found one of the great recipes to use them!

Preparing a meal is after a quest for the good life.

—**Eat My Words** by Janet Theophano

Makes 12 servings.
Per Serving: 235 Calories; 9g Fat (32.5% calories from fat); 4g Protein; 35g Carbohydrate; 1g Dietary Fiber; 39mg Cholesterol; 326mg Sodium.

Flame-Glazed Pineapple

1	large pineapple
1	tablespoon sugar
1/4	cup water – hot

1. Cut the top from the fresh pineapple. Make a 1/4 inch slice across the bottom to steady the pineapple on a solid base. From the top of the pineapple, make long cuts from top to bottom deep enough to strip away the peel. Follow around the pineapple, removing all spikes and undesirable pieces. Cut the pineapple in half from top to bottom. Take the first half and lay it flat surface down. Cut into at least four wedges lengthwise (large pineapples may yield six) keeping a piece of the core with each. Repeat with other half. Lay all pieces flat on a towel or paper towels and pat lightly to absorb extra juice.
2. Dissolve sugar in the hot water. Using a pastry brush, gently glaze the pineapple pieces on both sides. Place on a wax paper surface.
3. Using tongs, place the wedges over the coals. Watch carefully for flame ups from the sugar mixture. Turn after 1–2 minutes. Remove from heat when the wedges have the grill marks, give slightly when grasped with tongs, and are warmed throughout. These are delicious served alone, or over a small dish of ice cream.

These have the best flavor when prepared over charcoal. At the beginning of your grilling session, when the coals have just become hot, sizzle these and then remove them before cooking the meat. This will add flavor to your meat, and not risk raw meat juices on the pineapple.

Bad men live that they may eat and drink, whereas good men eat and drink that they may live.

—Socrates

Makes 4 servings.
Per Serving: 70 Calories; 1g Fat (5.9% calories from fat); trace Protein; 18g Carbohydrate; 1g Dietary Fiber; 0mg Cholesterol; 2mg Sodium.

Radical Radicchio
Accordion Tomato
Mango
Jicama Slaw
Salade Pamplemousse rose, Avocat et Crevettes

Don't Leaf Me Alone

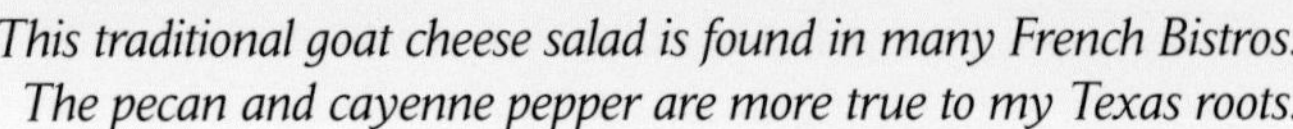

This traditional goat cheese salad is found in many French Bistros. The pecan and cayenne pepper are more true to my Texas roots.

Chèvre Rôti avec Rocket

1 bunch arugula – washed and trimmed
1 head Bibb lettuce – washed and trimmed
6 ounces goat cheese, sliced into 6 rounds
6 bacon slices – (thin sliced)
6 pecan halves
6 dashes cayenne pepper
1/2 cup extra virgin olive oil
1/4 cup salad vinegar
2 cloves garlic – minced
6 basil leaves – chiffonnade
salt and pepper – to taste

1. Preheat oven to 350F.
2. Wash greens and shake dry. Tear into bite sized pieces in a large bowl, toss together. Set in refrigerator to chill.
3. Take goat cheese and wrap with one slice of bacon, completely covering the cheese. Place wrapped cheese on a cookie sheet. Put one pecan half on top of each, and add a dash of cayenne on top of the pecan. Put in oven for 10–15 minutes until bacon begins to crisp. [Note: If thicker bacon is used, it may take 20–25 minutes in the oven.]
4. Put vinegar and garlic into a mixing bowl. Drizzle olive oil into the vinegar slowly, while beating mixture with a wire whisk until all the oil is incorporated. Add the basil, salt and very little pepper. (Arugula tastes peppery.)
5. Remove greens from refrigerator, and pour on the dressing. Toss until the mixture lightly covers the leaves.
6. Portion the salad onto plates, and place one warm goat cheese wrap on top of each salad. Serve.

Ready to branch out? Experiment with different flavored vinegars and oils!

Makes 6 servings.
Per Serving: 341 Calories; 32g Fat (84.1% calories from fat); 11g Protein; 3g Carbohydrate; 35mg Cholesterol; 201mg Sodium.

To chiffonnade basil: Stack a few leaves and roll them up from the side like a cigarette. Slice thinly to create small curly tendrils.

Try putting on latex gloves to truly toss the salad with your hands, and to serve it on the plates. I find it significantly easier.

Be very deliberate in wrapping the bacon around the cheese, as you don't want it to ooze out in baking.

What now?

So you wrapped it tight and the cheese leaked out anyway? Or, oops, it stayed in the oven a little too long and mostly melted?

Lay the bacon/cheese piece on a cutting board, and using a sharp tipped knife, score around the cheese and fold the melted portion under. Place gently on the salad. Voila!

A non-refrigerated option for an outdoor picnic!

German Coleslaw

1 large cabbage – shredded
1 onion
1 carrot
1 large green pepper
1 cup sugar
1 cup vinegar
2 Tablespoons dry mustard
2 Tablespoons celery seed
1 Tablespoon poppy seeds
1 teaspoon salt

1. Shred the onion, carrot and pepper on a grating board or box. Place all shredded ingredients into a large bowl and toss to combine.
2. Measure the sugar into a medium bowl. While pouring in the vinegar, whisk to dissolve the sugar. Add the remaining ingredients and mix thoroughly.
3. Pour the liquid mixture over the slaw and refrigerate overnight to combine the flavors.

The vinegar creates a tartness for the slaw that almost eliminates the need for salt. If you are watching your sodium intake, it can be easily eliminated. Buying packages of shredded vegetables makes this easy for anyone.

Our family has both German and French roots. This coleslaw was savored for its lack of mayonnaise.

"Recipe books allude to meals and events, people and places, successes and failures, joys and sorrows, lives and deaths of those loved and known. In sum, they represent the life worlds, past and present, of their creators."

— ***Eat My Words: Reading Women's Lives through the Cookbooks They Wrote,*** by Janet Theophano

Makes 10 servings.
Per Serving: 107 Calories; 1g Fat (8.3% calories from fat); 1g Protein; 25g Carbohydrate; 1g Dietary Fiber; 0mg Cholesterol; 221mg Sodium.

What I love best about this recipe is that the plates can be put on the table before the dinner party guests arrive, and then the dressing is added just before everyone is seated.

Accordion Tomato

1 large tomato
1 hard-boiled egg – peeled
1 piece leaf lettuce
1 Tablespoon creamy buttermilk salad dressing

1. Place tomato, core side down, on the cutting board. Starting on the right side of the tomato, make a slice toward the core to about 1/2 inch from the base of the tomato. Continue making slices into the tomato like a rainbow, 6 times. Gently open each slice, being careful not to break into the core.
2. Cut the hard-boiled egg from end to end into six slices. (An egg slicer makes this an easy job.) Place an egg slice into each opening of the tomato.
3. Arrange a lettuce leaf on a salad plate. Place the red and white striped tomato on top. Using about a tablespoon of creamy bottled dressing, pour an arch over the tomato and serve.

The substitution of fresh mozzarella cheese instead of the hard-boiled egg cries out for a creamy basil dressing.

You can remove the egg yolk to easily lower the total cholesterol count. Perhaps use a fat free dressing, too?

What now?
Slip of the knife: Slide the wedge back into the tomato or remove it and nestle a slightly larger piece of egg in its place

Makes 1 serving.
Per Serving: 242 Calories; 15g Fat (51.6% calories from fat); 13g Protein; 18g Carbohydrate; 9g Dietary Fiber; 213mg Cholesterol; 302mg Sodium.

When you are looking for a variety in the color of what you serve, try this salad.

Orange-Onion Salad

- 4 medium oranges – seedless
- 1 small red onion, thinly sliced into rings
- 5 Tablespoons dry white wine
- 1 clove garlic – minced
- 2 teaspoons tarragon vinegar – or other flavored vinegar
- 2 Tablespoons olive oil
- 4 lettuce leaves – large
- 2 green onions – chopped
- salt and pepper – to taste

1. Peel oranges and slice horizontally. Mix with sliced rings of red onion in a large mixing bowl.
2. In a small bowl, stir together the wine, garlic and vinegar. Drizzle olive oil into the mixture and whisk to combine. Pour over the orange and onion mixture. Allow to marinate at room temperature for at least 15 minutes.
3. Place orange-onion combination on a lettuce leaf and top with the chopped green onions. Serve.

Red leaf lettuce also looks beautiful with this salad. These deep rich colors signify the bundles of nutrients you are providing to your body.

"A gourmet is not, by definition, a studied epicure, a food snob. A gourmet is simply a person who cares about what he eats, such as a connoisseur in the delicacies of the table. Any good food is a delicacy, and anyone who seeks it out is a connoisseur. Why can't we all be gourmets, and proud of it — confident and hungry!

— by Coleman Andrews, executive editor of **Saveur**

Makes 4 servings.
Per Serving: 138 Calories; 5g Fat (34.9% calories from fat); 2g Protein; 20g Carbohydrate; 4g Dietary Fiber; 0mg Cholesterol; 14mg Sodium.

In honor of one of my teaching locations on Rawlins Street.

Pear Rawlins

6	large Bartlett pears – about 2 pounds
2	cups red wine – * see note
1/3	cup sugar
1/3	cup lemon juice – 1 large fresh lemon
2	teaspoons lemon zest – 1/2 large fresh lemon
2	Tablespoons sour cream
8	ounces blue cheese – Deep Ellum Blue
6	lettuce leaves

1. Gently peel the pears, using either a paring knife or a vegetable peeler. Starting at the base of the pear, insert a corer and remove all the seeds. Guard closely that you do not go so far up to damage the stem on top. A melon baller may also be used to remove more of the stringy stem where the pear bulges out.
2. Mix the wine, sugar, lemon juice and zest in a pot large enough to hold all pears standing up. There should be enough liquid to significantly cover the neck of the pears up to the base of the stem. Add as little water as required if there is not enough.
3. Bring the liquid to a gentle boil. Cover and simmer for about 15 minutes or a bit more if the pears are still hard.
4. Transfer the pears to a bowl, and move to refrigerator to chill.
5. Reduce the remaining liquid to about 2/3 cup, or until the liquid is a syrup-like consistency. (This may take about 20 minutes to reduce.) Remove from heat, add the sour cream and whisk vigorously. Chill sauce.
6. Divide the cheese into six equal portions. Press cheese into the opening of the pear and stuff them as full as possible.
7. When ready to serve, please one lettuce leaf on each plate and stand the pear upright. Drizzle 1–2 tablespoons of the sauce over the pear and serve.

* Full-bodied Beaujolais, Cote du Rhone, Gamay or Red Zinfandel may be used.

This is nice to have on the table before your dinner guests arrive. Drizzle the sauce over the pears just before everyone is seated.

Deep Ellum Blue is a very mild blue cheese that I love to use as an entry point for folks who claim they don't like blue cheese. After they have tried this, they are usually converted and searching for a cheese knife. Available at www.mozzco.com.

What now?
If the pears are damaged in peeling, coring or stuffing, just slice them into a fan pattern and place on the lettuce. I won't tell.

Makes 6 servings.
Per Serving: 341 Calories; 32g Fat (84.1% calories from fat); 11g Protein; 3g Carbohydrate; 35mg Cholesterol; 201mg Sodium.

An absolute favorite for a heat-safe picnic!

Mango Jicama Slaw

- 2 large mango – 1/2-inch cubes
- 1 large jicama – sliced 1/4 inch matchstick
- 1 cup sweet red pepper – sliced 1/4 inch matchstick
- 1/2 cup yellow bell pepper – sliced 1/4 inch matchstick
- 1/2 cup grated carrots
- 1/2 cup red onion – 1/4-inch dice
- 1/4 cup cilantro – chopped
- 1 jalapeño chile (1 to 2) – seeded and finely chopped
- 2 limes – juiced
- salt to taste

1. To cut the mango, hold it pointing up and slice just to the right and left of the large seed. Use great care because the cut mango is very slippery and the juice will stain. Lay the cut mango half skin side down, and score it in 1/2 inch cubes, being careful not to pierce the skin. Lift the mango half from the board and push on the skin side to make the squares of fruit protrude in a porcupine-like fashion. Using a sharp knife, slice down the skin and remove perfectly diced mango. Place into a large bowl. Repeat with the other half and the remaining mango.
2. Add jicama and peppers to the bowl. Stir in the grated carrot, diced red onion and cilantro. The mango juice will start to soften the vegetables as you finish preparations.
3. Wearing a latex glove on your non-knife hand, securely hold the jalapenos to seed and finely chop. Add to the bowl.
4. Juice the limes and toss all ingredients to combine. Taste to determine if salt is needed.
5. Cover and refrigerate for at least 30 minutes to blend flavors.

How to cut into matchstick pieces: Cut vegetables into 1/4 inch by 1/4 inch slices. Cut the pieces into 2 inch lengths to resemble the size of a matchstick.

Low in calories and 100% of your Vitamin A & C for the day make this recipe a winner! The jalapeno and lime kick give it a great boost.

What now?
No kidding on that mango juice stain. Soak it in cold water and get it in the wash as soon as possible. For me, I just go confess to my local cleaners and let them handle it.

Makes 8 servings. Yield: 2 1/2 cups
Per Serving: 88 Calories; trace Fat (3.5% calories from fat); 2g Protein; 22g Carbohydrate; 6g Dietary Fiber; 0mg Cholesterol; 10mg Sodium.

Radical Radicchio

1 head Radicchio – roughly chopped
6 romaine lettuce leaves – roughly chopped
10 pepperoncini peppers – finely chopped
15 Kalamata olives – finely chopped
1 Tablespoon fresh oregano – finely chopped
2 Tablespoons fresh basil – finely chopped
8 ounces mozzarella cheese – cubed
1 pint cherry tomatoes
2 Tablespoons salad vinegar
1 garlic clove – minced
1/4 cup extra virgin olive oil
2 cups Italian bread – cut in 1 inch cubes
Salt and pepper, to taste

1. Place all bite sized lettuce pieces in a large vegetable bag. Set in refrigerator to chill.
2. Mix together the pepperoncini, Kalamatas, oregano and basil with the cubed mozzarella in a large salad bowl.
3. In a small mixing bowl, combine vinegar and garlic. Drizzle olive oil into the vinegar slowly, while beating mixture with a wire whisk until all the oil is incorporated. Add salt and very little pepper.
4. When ready to serve, remove the lettuces from the refrigerator, and place in the large salad bowl with the olive mixture. Slowly pour the dressing on the leaves. Toss the combination together with the cherry tomatoes.
5. Let mixture stand while preparing the bread. Remove all crust from the bread, and cut into cubes. The bread will be very soft.
6. Toss bread cubes in with salad and serve immediately.

What now?
Truly serve immediately. This dish cannot be served as leftovers unless you are able to remove all the bread. It quickly becomes soggy as it absorbs the vinegar-rich dressing.

The Bienvenue-Montparnasse metro station is not just offering you a warm welcome. It is named after Fulgence Bienvenue (1852-1936), the one-armed engineer responsible for building the Paris Métro which opened in July of 1900.

Makes 8 servings.
Per Serving: 340 Calories; 17g Fat (45.7% calories from fat); 12g Protein; 34g Carbohydrate; 2g Dietary Fiber; 25mg Cholesterol; 469mg Sodium.

Vary the amount of peppercorns from 2 teaspoons up to almost 2 tablespoons for a cracker with a kick.

Other whole grains can be used, such as wheat or wheat berries. Additional plain flour may be necessary if other grains are used.

What now?
Humidity in the air will vary the cooking time on these crackers more than you can imagine. Keep using the 'bend' test. When it comes time to break them apart, the irregular shapes are the hallmark of homemade.

"The living of life is more important than the necessary pieces of it. Do you want to look back on your time in Paris and say that the laundry was always finished?"

— Gretchen Leach, wife of the US Ambassador to France speaking to the new arrival of English speaking ex-pats to Paris.

These crackers make an excellent accompaniment for many of the salads in this chapter.

Pepper-Rye Crackers

- 3/4 cup rye – whole grain
- 1 1/2 cups water
- 1 cup rye flour
- 1/2 cup all-purpose flour
- 1/2 teaspoon baking powder
- 1/2 teaspoon salt
- 4 Tablespoons unsalted butter – softened
- 1/2 cup buttermilk
- 1 Tablespoon whole black peppercorns
- 1/2 teaspoon Kosher salt

1. Preheat oven to 300F.
2. Place whole grain rye and water in a saucepan and cook until the rye is soft and all liquid has been absorbed. Allow to cool while preparing other ingredients.
3. Place black peppercorns in food processor and pulse a few times to break into small pieces. Add the flours, baking powder and regular salt to a large mixing bowl using a fork to blend.
4. While the mixer is running on low speed, add cooked rye, buttermilk and butter to the flour mixture. Once the dough has formed a soft ball, remove the dough from the mixer.
5. Turn the dough onto a lightly floured surface. Roll to the thickness of the rye kernels and place on a cookie sheet. Score the crackers, and use a fork to aerate the cracker to rise evenly. Sprinkle with Kosher salt.
6. Bake for approximately 15–20 minutes. Check on crackers at 15 minutes. If the cracker bends easily, bake the additional 5 minutes. Remove to a wire rack. Once cooled, break apart into pieces and store in an airtight container.

Makes 20 servings.
Per Serving: 74 Calories; 3g Fat (30.9% calories from fat); 2g Protein; 11g Carbohydrate; 1g Dietary Fiber; 6mg Cholesterol; 120mg Sodium.

Texas Ruby Red Grapefruit makes this dish outstanding.

Salade Pamplemousse rose, Avocat et Crevettes

When I was invited to my neighbor's home for dinner in Saint Cloud, France, a similar salad graced the table just before we were seated. The colors were vibrant and the flavor delicious. I recall that delightful party each time I prepare this dish.

If you have trouble finding arugula, another dark green lettuce will also work well, but add pepper to the salad. Bibb lettuce can be substituted for the Lamb's Ear, but it's worth a little search to have this ingredient.

You want to have at least two pieces of shrimp and four pieces of avocado and grapefruit per salad. If the avocado is not large enough, cut one more.

1 quart water – salted
8 ounces shrimp – 16/18 count, peeled, tails remaining
3 ounces fresh ginger – peeled and sliced
1 teaspoon cayenne pepper
8 ounces yogurt, low fat
2 Tablespoons orange juice
1 teaspoon spicy brown mustard
1/2 teaspoon dark sesame oil
salt and pepper
8 ounces Lamb's lettuce (or Bibb lettuce)
5 ounces arugula (or baby spinach)
1 large pink grapefruit – peeled and sectioned
1 large avocado – cut in 1/2 inch slices
8 pieces pickled ginger

1. Bring the salted water and ginger to a low boil. Add shrimp and cook for 1–2 minutes until shrimp turns pink. Remove pot from heat and tap the cayenne into the water. As you lift the shrimp from the pot with a slotted spoon, some of the cayenne will stick and add flavor. Place shrimp on a plate. Cover and chill.
2. Whisk together the yogurt, juice, mustard, sesame oil, salt and pepper in a small bowl. Cover and chill.
3. Rinse lettuces and lightly roll in towels to crisp. Place in refrigerator until serving time.
4. To serve, toss the lettuces in the yogurt dressing and arrange on 8 plates. Place one shrimp vertically, tail up, on the right and left side of the salad. Alternate the avocado and grapefruit around the sides, distributing evenly. Gently twist the pickled ginger and place between the shrimp tails on the top.

Makes 8 servings.
Per Serving: 142 Calories; 5g Fat (33.0% calories from fat); 9g Protein; 15g Carbohydrate; 3g Dietary Fiber; 44mg Cholesterol; 77mg Sodium.

Don't take flash pictures at night from a cab in a major European city. It looks too much like the police speed camera's flash to your taxi driver. Perhaps you should warn them first.

What now?

If you can see ripples in the oil, it is too hot and will 'cook' your vinegar dressing. Let it cool a bit to the touch.

Warm Broccoli Slaw

10 ounces broccoli slaw – packaged
1 cup onion – finely chopped
2 carrots – finely chopped
1/2 cup cilantro – finely chopped
1/2 cup red wine vinegar
2 Tablespoons dry mustard
1 garlic clove – minced
2 teaspoons sugar
1 teaspoon salt
1/3 cup safflower oil

1. In a large bowl, combine the broccoli slaw, onion, carrot, and cilantro.
2. In a medium bowl, mix together the vinegar, dry mustard, garlic, sugar and salt.
3. In a small saucepan, gently heat the oil. When a drop of heated oil on the counter feels warm to the touch, remove from heat. Whisking quickly, drizzle the warm oil into the vinegar bowl until it is all incorporated.
4. Pour the dressing over the slaw and toss to blend. Serve immediately while warm.

This is an excellent side dish with pork chops.

Makes 8 servings.
Per Serving: 118 Calories; 10g Fat (69.1% calories from fat); 2g Protein; 8g Carbohydrate; 2g Dietary Fiber; 0mg Cholesterol; 283mg Sodium.

Mango Chile Puree

Red Chile-Yogurt Sauce

Lemon Herb Butter

Barbeque Rub

Dressin' Up Your Saucy Ways

Presto Pesto

1 1/2	cups basil leaves – torn and tough stems removed
3/4	cup pine nuts – toasted
1	clove garlic
1/2	teaspoon salt
1/4	teaspoon pepper
1/2	cup olive oil

1. Place all ingredients except oil in a blender or food processor. Pulse on and off until chopped.
2. Slowly add the oil in a steady stream. Continue to mix until smooth.
3. Sauce can be refrigerated or frozen. Makes approximately one cup.

Other combinations can include Bok Choy, cilantro or spinach with pecans, almonds or hazelnuts.

Serve over pasta, as a pizza base instead of tomato sauce, or with Les Tomates Étreintes.

Makes 16 servings.
Per Serving: 113 Calories; 10g Fat (75.2% calories from fat); 3g Protein; 5g Carbohydrate; 3g Dietary Fiber; 0mg Cholesterol; 69mg Sodium.

"May you always have old memories and young hopes."
Ancient Blessing

Mango Chile Puree

2 mangoes – peeled and sliced
2 Tablespoons roasted red chile paste
2 Tablespoons lime juice – about 1 lime
1 bunch cilantro – stems and leaves separated
3 Tablespoons olive oil
1 yellow bell pepper, 1/4 inch dice

1. Peel and loosely slice the mangoes. Add peeled mangoes to a food processor and pulse a few times to roughly chop.
2. Add chili paste, lime juice, cilantro stems (reserve leaves) to the processor and mix until smooth. Drizzle in the olive oil until it is completely incorporated.
3. Remove puree from the processor and stir in the diced yellow bell peppers. Refrigerate until ready to use. Garnish with the fresh cilantro leaves.

*Heat may be regulated by adding more or less chili paste. This version is quite spicy and delicious with tenderloin. I recommend **one** Tablespoon of the chili paste for serving with poultry or fish.*

Makes 12 servings.
Per Serving: 64 Calories; 4g Fat (52.5% calories from fat); 1g Protein; 7g Carbohydrate; 1g Dietary Fiber; 1mg Cholesterol; 23mg Sodium.

Lemon Herb Butter

1/2 cup unsalted butter – (1 stick)
3 Tablespoons fresh herbs – (basil, dill or sage)
1 Tablespoon lemon juice
1 teaspoon Dijon-style mustard
1 teaspoon lemon zest

1. Whip the butter until smooth with an electric mixer. Add the remaining ingredients, and stir until well combined. Refrigerate.

The original St. Cloud, near Paris, France, was the place where Napoleon's family lived. It was named after the grandson of the first Christian King of France.

When using sage, this butter really adds to cornbread and fresh dinner rolls.

Makes 12 servings.
Per Serving: 69 Calories; 8g Fat (97.1% calories from fat); trace Protein; trace Carbohydrate; trace Dietary Fiber; 21mg Cholesterol; 8mg Sodium.

Refreshing sauce for lighter fish, such as tilapia or sole

Fennel-Yogurt Sauce

- 8 ounces plain lowfat yogurt
- 2 Tablespoons lime juice, (1/2 lime)
- 1/2 cup fennel ferns – or dill
- 1 clove garlic – minced

1. Spoon four ounces of yogurt in a blender. Combine all other ingredients and mix well. Add remaining yogurt, and stir until smooth. Refrigerate.

Fennel is a celery-like vegetable found easily in the fall. The frilly ferns are on top. During the other seasons, you can substitute dill for the fennel ferns.

Susan J. Leonardi has pointed out that the (recipe) exchange appears to be a way for women to cross boundaries of race, class, region and generation. She recognizes that recipes and food lore contribute a realm of activity that connects women despite differences. The Latin word 'recipere' means exchange, and women have seen recipes as tokens in a gift relationship.

— **Eat My Words: Reading Women's Lives through the Cookbooks They Wrote**
by Janet Theophano

Makes 8 servings.
Per Serving: 21 Calories; trace Fat (18.4% calories from fat); 2g Protein; 3g Carbohydrate; trace Dietary Fiber; 2mg Cholesterol; 23mg Sodium.

The cayenne pepper gives this the essence of its heat. Increase or reduce to your liking.

Kevin Garvin shared this recipe while working the best 'real' job he has ever known—being The Chef

Barbeque Rub

- 1/4 cup salt
- 1/4 cup sugar
- 1/4 cup brown sugar
- 1/4 cup cumin
- 1/4 cup chili powder
- 1/4 cup black pepper
- 1/4 cup paprika
- 2 Tablespoons cayenne pepper

1. Mix all ingredients together with a fork. Keep in a dry, airtight container. Makes almost 2 cups.

*Try specialty chili powders for a variation.
Ancho chiles and chipotle are delicious for pork.*

Makes 30 servings.
Per Serving: 23 Calories; 1g Fat (18.3% calories from fat); 1g Protein; 5g Carbohydrate; 1g Dietary Fiber; 0mg Cholesterol; 865mg Sodium.

We live our lives one of three ways, treadmill, saga, or pilgrimage. Take your pick, for it is a choice you must make everyday.

— **Gutsy Women**
by Marybeth Bond

Ruby Pepper Sauce

1 1/2 cups grapefruit juice — (2 grapefruit, juiced)
2 cups orange juice — (6 oranges, juiced)
2 Tablespoons lemon juice – (1 small lemon, juiced)
2 serrano peppers — seeded and chopped
1 jalapeño pepper — seeded and chopped
3 Tablespoons mint leaves — chopped
1 Tablespoon oregano — chopped
1/2 cup unsalted butter — (1 stick)
1 teaspoon salt

1. Pour all the fresh-squeezed juices into a saucepan. Whisk over high heat until reduced to about 1/2 cup of liquid. Add the peppers and herbs, cover and let the flavors infuse for about 20 minutes.
2. Strain the mixture, removing the pulp, peppers, and herb leaves. Pour back into the saucepan, and bring to a slow simmer. Add the softened butter, one Tablespoon at a time, and whisk until it is completely incorporated.
3. Add salt and adjust seasonings, if neccessary.

Drizzle a little over steamed vegetables, or use as a dipping sauce for grilled shrimp.

Makes 8 servings.
Per Serving: 152 Calories; 12g Fat (67.4% calories from fat); 1g Protein; 12g Carbohydrate; 1g Dietary Fiber; 31mg Cholesterol; 270mg Sodium.

Pour this over coleslaw mix and you will find it is a whole new salad!

Warm Poppyseed-Rosemary Dressing

- 1/3 cup sugar
- 1/4 cup rice wine vinegar
- 1/2 teaspoon salt
- 1 Tablespoon cocktail onions – juice only
- 1/2 teaspoon dry mustard
- 1/2 cup vegetable oil
- 1 Tablespoon poppy seeds
- 1 Tablespoon fresh rosemary – chopped

1. In a medium saucepan, stir together sugar, vinegar, salt, onion juice, and dry mustard. Gently simmer over low heat until the sugar dissolves.
2. Adding oil in a slow stream, whisk into the warm mixture until all oil is emulsified. Mixture will start to foam heavily if the heat is too high. Remove from heat momentarily, if necessary.
3. When all the oil is incorporated, add the poppy seeds and rosemary. Stir.

Our appetite should always be larger and more curious than our hunger.

— John Thorne, ***Perfect Food***

Makes 12 servings.
Per Serving: 107 Calories; 9g Fat (77.3% calories from fat); trace Protein; 6g Carbohydrate; trace Dietary Fiber; 0mg Cholesterol; 98mg Sodium.

The Rosemary-Poppyseed Dressing was created just for this dish.

Gondola Salad

6	whole cucumbers – 6-8 inches long
2	cups green bell pepper – 1/4 inch dice
1 1/2	cups fresh corn – cut from cob
1/2	cup red bell pepper – 1/4 inch dice
1 1/2	cups mango – 1/4 inch dice
3/4	cup cucumber – (*see step 1)
3	cups radicchio – shredded

1. Rinse cucumbers. Peel the green skin lengthwise from the front one-third of the cucumber. Being careful not to cut through the whole vegetable, make a one inch horizontal slice through the skinned section, about 3/4 inch to one inch from the top. On each side, cut down into a "V" pattern, meeting about 3/4 inch to 1 inch from the opposite end. Remove the cucumber section and all internal seeds. This will resemble an open canoe. Reserve the white section of the cucumber for step 3.
2. Combine corn and peppers in a large bowl.
3. Using the removed, white, seeded sections of cucumber, cut into 1/4 inch slices and dice. Reserve excess for use in another recipe. Combine mango and cucumber in a small bowl.
4. After the addition of the herbs and while the Rosemary-Poppyseed dressing is still hot, pour the bowl of peppers and corn into the dressing. Stir gently to coat for about two minutes to remove the raw bell pepper taste.
5. Turn all chopped ingredients and dressing into a large bowl and toss to coat.
6. Place the empty cucumber gondolas in the center of each plate. Dividing the vegetable mixture evenly among the plates, fill the gondolas using a slotted spoon.
7. Add the shredded radicchio into the remaining dressing and toss lightly to coat. Spoon dressed radicchio on each side of the 'boats' to keep them upright. Serve immediately while the dressing is still warm.

If preparing in advance, cut all vegetables and place in two bowls at step 7. Cover and refrigerate; continue just before serving.

Makes 8 servings.
Per Serving: 122 Calories; 1g Fat (7.3% calories from fat); 4g Protein; 28g Carbohydrate; 6g Dietary Fiber; 0mg Cholesterol; 19mg Sodium.

Looks beautiful on the holiday buffet.

Spinach Salad Dressing

- 1/2 cup sugar
- 1/4 cup vinegar
- 1/2 cup sesame oil
- 1/2 cup vegetable oil
- 1 Tablespoon Worcestershire sauce
- 1 Tablespoon soy sauce, low sodium
- 1 teaspoon salt
- 1/2 cup onion – grated finely

1. In a medium bowl, combine the sugar and vinegar. Slowly drizzle in the oils and whisk to emulsify.
2. Add the Worchestershire, soy sauce and salt. Add the onion and blend all ingredients together.
3. Pour the dressing over the spinach salad about 10 minutes before serving and toss to combine. This allows the spinach leaves to absorb the flavors.

Toss the salad with mandarin oranges and slivered almonds. Place a few red onion rings on top to serve. Thank you Aunt Dorothy.

Your own personal epiphany. Christmas reveals itself to each of us in a personal way — be it secular or sacred. Whatever Christmas is — and it's many things to many people — we all own a piece of it. Kinda like Santa's bag — inside there's a gift for everyone.

— **Chris In The Morning** of **Northern Exposure**

Makes 16 servings.
Per Serving: 148 Calories; 14g Fat (80.8% calories from fat); trace Protein; 7g Carbohydrate; trace Dietary Fiber; 0mg Cholesterol; 180mg Sodium.

Serve with fish as a spicy and cool addition.

Red Chile-Yogurt Sauce

- 8 ounces plain lowfat yogurt
- 1 Tablespoon roasted red chile paste
- 1 teaspoon honey
- 1/2 teaspoon cinnamon

1. Spoon four ounces of yogurt in a blender. Combine all other ingredients and mix well. Add remaining yogurt, and stir until smooth. Refrigerate.

Recipe Roulette: For some of us, entertaining is the same as playing the lottery or entering the Publisher's Clearing House Sweepstakes. A dinner party is just an excuse to try out at least one new, complicated recipe, if not a whole menu. For me and cooks like me — dinner parties have all the dangerous excitement of Russian roulette. They're not so much about eating as they are about entertainment.

— Kit Snedoker, food Editor of
Los Angeles Herald Examiner

Makes 8 servings.
Per Serving: 27 Calories; 1g Fat (26.6% calories from fat); 2g Protein; 3g Carbohydrate; trace Dietary Fiber; 2mg Cholesterol; 36mg Sodium.

Tomate et Courgette Escalier
Flame-Glazed Pineapple
Speckled Blue Marlin on the Thai High Seas

Meat Of The Matter

Don't Chicken Out

Fishing for Compliments

Chicken
Grandly on the Throne

Serve with Pico de Gallo and steamed zucchini for a flavorful and healthful meal.

Caliente Crusted Chicken

You have the option of varying the crushed corn flakes to another cereal. If using one of the high fiber wheat flake cereals, I find that doubling the amount of dried spice amounts will achieve the recipe's original flavor.

- 1 cup vegetable juice cocktail – extra spicy
- 2 pounds skinless chicken breast halves
- 2 ounces cheddar cheese – shredded
- 1/3 cup corn flakes – crushed
- 1 garlic clove – minced
- 1 teaspoon oregano
- 1 teaspoon cumin
- 1/2 teaspoon chili powder
- 1/2 teaspoon paprika
- 1/2 teaspoon salt
- 1/2 teaspoon pepper

1. In a large re-sealable plastic bag, or a shallow non-aluminum dish, combine vegetable juice and chicken. Place chicken with the meat side down in the juice. Marinate for 20–30 minutes at room temperature, or 3 hours in the refrigerator.
2. Preheat oven to 375F. Drain chicken and discard the marinade. Prepare a baking sheet with non-stick cooking spray.
3. Combine all remaining ingredients in a shallow bowl or pie plate. Dip chicken into the corn flake mixture, coating the meat side thoroughly. Place on baking sheet. Sprinkle any remaining crumb mixture over the chicken.
4. Bake for 1 hour, until chicken is crisp and golden. Timing will be approximately 40 minutes if using boneless breasts.

Makes 6 servings.
Per Serving: 189 Calories; 5g Fat (23.8% calories from fat); 31g Protein; 4g Carbohydrate; 1g Dietary Fiber; 80mg Cholesterol; 443mg Sodium.

Every Mother's dream: quick, healthy, colorful and filling!

Chicken with Tomatoes and Yellow Squash

4 boneless skinless chicken breasts
Salt and pepper
2 Tablespoons oil
1 cup onion – cut in 1/2 inch dice
2 cloves garlic – minced
2 yellow squash – cut in 1 inch pieces
8 ounces mushrooms – quartered
15 ounces canned tomatoes – diced
2 serrano peppers – cut in 1/4 inch dice

1. Place the chicken breasts between two pieces of plastic wrap, or inside a large resealable bag. Using a large mallet, pound breasts to 1/2 inch thickness. Pat dry and lightly season with salt and pepper.
2. Heat oil in a large skillet. Brown chicken and remove to a plate.
3. Sauté onion and garlic until onion is translucent. Add squash and mushrooms to the pan. Cook for about 3 minutes.
4. Add chicken back to the pan. Pour tomatoes over the chicken and add serranos.
5. Cover and simmer over low heat about 20 minutes until chicken is tender.

"If more of us valued food and cheer and song above hoarded gold, it would be a merrier world."

— JRR Tolkien

Makes 4 servings.
Per Serving: 384 Calories; 10g Fat (24.4% calories from fat); 58g Protein; 14g Carbohydrate; 4g Dietary Fiber; 137mg Cholesterol; 316mg Sodium.

The crushed pineapple topping creates a juicy and moist chicken.

Hawaiian Chicken

- 4 skinless chicken breasts
- 4 Tablespoons low sodium soy sauce
- 1/2 teaspoon coriander
- 8 ounces crushed pineapple in juice
- 1 red bell pepper – cut in 1/2 inch strips

1. Preheat oven to 325F.
2. Rinse chicken breasts, and pat dry. Arrange evenly in a glass dish, without crowding.
3. Using a table fork, pierce holes in the meat of the chicken breasts. Slowly pour one tablespoon of soy sauce over each breast, allowing the liquid to absorb. Add one dash of ground coriander to each breast.
4. Using a spoon, mound approximately 2 Tablespoons crushed pineapple over each breast, just covering the meat. Pour remaining juice from can into the dish to add moisture while cooking.
5. Place red bell pepper strips in a criss-cross fashion over the breasts.
6. Place dish in oven. Cook for approximately 25–30 minutes until the juices run clear.

After learning this recipe at a weight-loss group, I served it frequently over rice with steamed broccoli. Its classic simplicity added to its appeal.

Boneless breasts will bake about 20 minutes.

Makes 4 servings.
Per Serving: 311 Calories; 3g Fat (9.1% calories from fat); 56g Protein; 12g Carbohydrate; 1g Dietary Fiber; 137mg Cholesterol; 755mg Sodium.

After you delight with laughter over the title of this recipe, prepare to be delighted with the flavor of it as well!

Chicken Grandly on the Throne

5	pounds whole chicken
12	ounces beer – canned
1	lime
1	Tablespoon dry mustard
1/2	cup onion – cut in 1/2 inch pieces
2	serrano peppers – sliced lengthwise
2	Tablespoons seasoned salt
1	Tablespoon cumin – or smoked paprika
1 1/2	Tablespoons lemon juice

1. Prepare grill; let coals reach a temperature of 300F. Remove the giblets from the chicken, rinse, and pat dry. Salt and pepper the cavity. Set aside.
2. Open the beer can with a can opener and pour out half of the contents. (Drink it, or save it; see sidebar) Zest the entire lime, and place zest in a small glass dish. Slice the lime into three large chunks. With a straw, gently stir the dry mustard into the beer can. (It will froth, be careful.) Add chopped onion, serranos and limes to the can of beer. Open the cavity of the chicken wide, and gently slide the beer can inside. [If desired, place in a pan. An 8 inch or 9 inch round cake pan works best.]
3. Add the seasoned salt, cumin and lemon juice to the zest in the glass dish. Stir into a thick paste. Hand rub into the chicken, thoroughly.
4. Place chicken, upright on its throne, on the grill. Slow grill at 300F for about 2 hours, until the internal temperature of the thigh is 180F, or the breast is 165F on an instant read thermometer. Let rest for 10 minutes before carving.

Optional Mop:
If you choose to baste the chicken while it is smoking, the following mop is suggested. Baste after the second hour, and about once an hour after that, until 30 minutes before the chicken is ready.

6 ounces beer
1 teaspoon lemon zest
1 cup chicken stock
1 teaspoon cumin
3 Tablespoons corn or canola oil
1 teaspoon paprika

Makes 6 servings.
Per Serving: 600 Calories; 39g Fat (61.6% calories from fat); 49g Protein; 6g Carbohydrate; 1g Dietary Fiber; 235mg Cholesterol; 1555mg Sodium.

Beautiful as appetizer portions: Cut romaine leaves crosswise into 3 inch pieces and arrange them on a platter. Spoon a small amount of the chicken into each and serve.

If the chicken is slightly frozen, it's much easier to slice thinly

Pignoli Nut Chicken Wraps

1	pound boneless skinless chicken breasts – slightly frozen
2	teaspoons cornstarch
1	egg white
2	Tablespoons white wine
1/2	teaspoon salt
1/2	teaspoon sugar
8	large lettuce leaves – Bibb or Iceberg
3	Tablespoons oil
3	Tablespoons fresh ginger – finely shredded
3	serrano peppers – cut in 1/4 inch slivers
1	Tablespoon cornstarch
1/2	cup pine nuts – (pignoli) toasted

1. Slice chicken breast as thinly as possible, about 1/8 inch slices. Cut slices into 2 inch pieces. Place in a glass dish.
2. Sprinkle cornstarch over chicken. Toss lightly until coated. Add egg white, wine, salt and sugar. Stir to combine.
3. Separate the lettuce leaves. Rinse them under cold running water, and pat dry. Arrange on a serving platter, and refrigerate.
4. Heat oil in a skillet until ripples start to form in the oil. Quickly stir in the ginger, and cook for 30 seconds. Add chicken mixture. Stir-fry over moderate heat for one to two minutes or until all the chicken turns firm and white. Add peppers and stir to combine.
5. In a small dish, stir together 1 Tablespoon of cornstarch with 1 Tablespoon water. Add to chicken and stir to create a glaze. Remove from heat.
6. Place chicken mixture in a serving bowl and top with pignoli nuts. Serve with chilled lettuce leaves. Guests will spoon hot chicken mixture into leaves and wrap lengthwise.

Makes 4 servings.
Per Serving: 343 Calories; 20g Fat (54.1% calories from fat); 32g Protein; 7g Carbohydrate; 1g Dietary Fiber; 66mg Cholesterol; 358mg Sodium.

Turkey in the Bundt®

Creative use of leftovers award: Stuffing and Thanksgiving turkey, days later.

- 1 1/2 cups bread — toasted and crumbled
- 1/2 cup onion — cut in 1/2 inch dice
- 1/2 cup celery — cut in 1/2 inch dice
- 2 cups turkey — cooked and diced
- 2 cups Swiss cheese — shredded
- 1 1/2 cups bread — toasted and crumbled
- 4 eggs — beaten
- 2 1/2 cups milk
- 2 teaspoons thyme
- 1 teaspoon salt
- 1/2 teaspoon white pepper
- 1/4 teaspoon dry mustard
- 1/4 teaspoon poultry seasoning

1. Preheat oven to 350F.
2. Sprinkle 2 cups of the bread in the bottom of a greased Bundt® or fluted tube pan. Sprinkle the onions and celery over the bread. Distribute turkey evenly over the mixture. Spread cheese over the turkey. Top with the remaining 2 cups of bread.
3. In a medium bowl, combine beaten eggs with milk and dry seasonings. Pour over the mixture in the pan. Place tube pan inside a larger pan. A 13 inch x 9 inch pan works well. Fill the outer pan with water about halfway up the side of the tube pan. Bake for 45 minutes.
4. Remove tube pan from the water-filled dish and bake an additional 15 minutes, or until a knife inserted in the center comes out clean. Cool 10 minutes.
5. With a spatula, loosen the turkey mixture from the edges of the pan and invert onto a plate. Cut in slices and serve.

Principles have no real force except when one is well fed.

— Mark Twain

Makes 8 servings.
Per Serving: 509 Calories; 20g Fat (35.6% calories from fat); 31g Protein; 50g Carbohydrate; 3g Dietary Fiber; 175mg Cholesterol; 927mg Sodium.

Country Captain Chicken

- 3 pounds skinless chicken breasts
- 1/2 teaspoon salt
- 1/4 teaspoon pepper
- 2 Tablespoons flour
- 2 Tablespoons oil
- 1 1/2 cups onion – cut in 1/2 inch dice
- 3/4 cup carrots – cut in 1/2 inch dice
- 3/4 cup bell peppers – cut in 1/2 inch dice
- 2 cloves garlic – minced
- 1 Tablespoon curry powder
- 15 ounces canned tomatoes – diced
- 1/4 cup raisins
- 1/2 cup chicken broth

In the summer, harvest homegrown or heirloom tomatoes for a bold flavor.

1. Cut breasts into 4 inch pieces. Season with salt and pepper, then dust lightly with flour.
2. Heat oil in a large skillet. Add chicken and brown on all sides. Remove to a plate.
3. Sauté onion, carrot, bell pepper, and garlic in the skillet until tender. Add curry powder, tomatoes with their juice and raisins and stir to combine. Bring to a boil.
4. Return chicken to the pan and add the broth. Reduce heat, cover and simmer for 20 minutes. Remove cover and continue simmering until chicken is tender, about 5 to 10 minutes longer.

"Never argue at the dinner table, for the one who is not hungry gets the best of the argument."

— Richard Whately, theological writer

Makes 6 servings.
Per Serving: 316 Calories; 7g Fat (21.1% calories from fat); 44g Protein; 17g Carbohydrate; 3g Dietary Fiber; 105mg Cholesterol; 473mg Sodium.

Spicy curry and sweet coconut transport your taste buds straight to the islands.

Caribbean Crab Soufflé

If fresh crabmeat is unavailable, I prefer a high quality canned crabmeat, such as Phillips brand.

2	Tablespoons unsalted butter
1/2	cup celery – cut in 1/2 inch dice
1	clove garlic – minced
1/2	teaspoon curry powder
1/2	teaspoon dried thyme
1/2	teaspoon red pepper flakes
1/2	teaspoon salt
3	Tablespoons flour
1	cup milk
4	eggs
1/2	cup coconut – toasted
1/2	pound crab meat – cartilage removed
2	Tablespoons seasoned crackers – crumbled

1. Preheat the oven to 375F. Prepare an 8 cup souffle dish or glass deep-dish pie pan with non-stick spray. Set aside.
2. Melt butter in a large saucepan over low heat. Stir in the celery, garlic, curry powder, thyme, red pepper flakes, salt and pepper. Cook for 3 minutes.
3. Add the flour, and stir until smooth. Cook for 1 minute.
4. Add the milk, and cook over medium heat, stirring until the mixture comes to a boil and is thick and smooth. Set it aside to cool slightly.
5. Whisk the eggs in a small bowl. Stir in the coconut and crabmeat. Gently blend the crab into the saucepan mixture.
6. Pour mixture into the baking dish. Dust with cracker mixture and place it on a rack in the bottom third of the oven. Bake 30 minutes until puffed and golden. It may be still moist inside. Serve immediately.

Makes 8 servings.
Per Serving: 140 Calories; 8g Fat (52.5% calories from fat); 11g Protein; 5g Carbohydrate; 1g Dietary Fiber; 143mg Cholesterol; 286mg Sodium.

Serve on a large beautiful platter, and announce this dish with its English translation: Paella Bathed in Gold

Paella Lavé en Or

While mussels are traditional, clams can also be used.

- 1 pound mussels
- 1 pound andouille sausage — cut in 1 inch slices
- 3 leeks — cut in 1/2 inch slices
- 1/2 cup celery — cut in 1/2 inch dice
- 1 pound skinless chicken thighs
- 1 pound chicken wings — drumettes
- 2 teaspoons Herbes de Provence
- 1 teaspoon fresh ginger
- 15 ounces pineapple tidbits in juice
- 2 tomatoes — cut in 1/2 inch pieces
- 1 green bell pepper — cut in 1 inch pieces
- 2 cups long-grain rice
- 5 cloves garlic — minced
- 2 teaspoons salt
- 1 teaspoon pepper
- 1 teaspoon cayenne pepper
- 1 teaspoon saffron threads
- 2 cups chicken broth
- 3 cups water
- 1 large jalapeño
- 1 cup white wine
- 1 pound shrimp — 21–25 per pound, deveined
- 1 yellow bell pepper — cut in 1 inch pieces
- 1 cup frozen green peas

Makes 10 servings.
Per Serving: 375 Calories; 8g Fat (19.2% calories from fat); 30g Protein; 42g Carbohydrate; 3g Dietary Fiber; 122mg Cholesterol; 851mg Sodium.

As culinary leaders of our families, we are nourishing a generation to have a relationship with the stove.

1. Sort through the mussels and discard any that are open. Scrub remaining mussels and remove beards. Set aside in refrigerator.
2. Brown sausage in a large skillet and remove to a bowl.
3. Sauté leek and celery until leek has wilted. Cut chicken thighs into 1 inch pieces, and add with drumettes to skillet. Sauté, turning frequently for 4–5 minutes. Add Herbes de Provence, ginger and pineapple with the juice. Add up to 1/2 cup of water if mixture appears too dry. Cover and poach chicken for approximately 10 minutes to absorb the flavors.
4. Add tomato, green bell pepper, rice, garlic, salt, pepper, cayenne, saffron, and 2 cups broth. Stir generously to combine. Make 5–6 cuts in the jalapeño from stem to tip, keeping the stem intact. (Resembling a tulip) Add 3 cups water and float the jalapeño in the liquid. Cover and simmer 15–20 minutes, opening to stir once or twice.
5. Pour in the white wine. Stir in the shrimp, cooked sausage, yellow pepper and peas. Gently place the mussels around the dish. Cover and simmer until the shrimp turn pink and the mussels are open.
6. When ready to serve, discard any mussels that did not open. Serve in the skillet dish, or on a large platter.

Add a crisp, spicy white wine to complete this inviting al fresco dinner such as a New Zealand Sauvignon Blanc.

If the Kalamata olive flavor is too strong for you, any other type of black olive may be substituted.

Grilled Sicilian Swordfish

- 1 1/2 pounds swordfish steaks – approximately 6
- 1 Tablespoon olive oil
- 2 Tablespoons extra-virgin olive oil
- 1 1/2 cups onion – cut in 1/2 inch dice
- 4 cloves garlic – minced
- 1/2 teaspoon crushed red pepper
- 2 large tomatoes – cut in 1 inch dice
- 1/2 cup raisins
- 1/2 cup pine nuts (pignolia) – toasted
- 1/2 cup Kalamata olives – cut in fourths
- 1 Tablespoon Italian seasoning
- 1 cup Italian parsley – chopped

1. Prepare grill. Rinse fish and pat dry. Brush with olive oil and set aside.
2. Place each piece on the grill and cook for 6+3 minutes per inch. [This translates to: A 1 inch thick piece rests 6 minutes on the first side, and half the amount of time (3 minutes) on the other. Increase or decrease this time with the varying thickness.] Remove to the serving plate when complete.
3. Heat extra-virgin olive oil in a large skillet. Add diced onions, minced garlic, and crushed red pepper. Sauté until the onions start to turn golden, 3 to 4 minutes.
4. Add diced tomatoes, raisins, nuts, olives and Italian seasoning. Continue to sauté for 2–3 more minutes. The liquid from the tomatoes should begin to thicken.
5. Spread the chopped parsley like a blanket over the fish. Gently pour the hot tomato mixture over the parsley. Serve.

Makes 6 servings.
Per Serving: 382 Calories; 23g Fat (52.4% calories from fat); 27g Protein; 19g Carbohydrate; 3g Dietary Fiber; 44mg Cholesterol; 429mg Sodium.

The crab's scientific name is Callinectes sapidus *which means "beautiful swimmer." The biggest blue crab caught in Maryland was a male which measured 9 inches.*

Crab Quiche

1	pie shell – prepared
1/2	cup swiss cheese – grated
3	Tablespoons butter
1	Tablespoon green onion – chopped (green and white)
1	can crab meat – drained
1/4	teaspoon salt
1/2	teaspoon white pepper
2	tablespoons white wine
3	eggs – beaten
1	cup half and half

1. Preheat oven to 375F.
2. Prick the bottom of the pie shell with a fork and bake for 5 minutes. Cool slightly. Spread grated cheese in the bottom of the pie shell.
3. In a skillet, melt butter and sauté the green onions. Add the crab meat, salt and white pepper. Stir gently and heat through. Add wine and bring to a boil. Remove from heat and allow to cool.
4. In a medium bowl, beat the eggs. Add half and half and gradually blend in crab mixture. Pour crab mixture over the cheese in the pie shell. Bake for 25 to 30 minutes, or until a knife inserted in the center comes out clean.

The primary requisite for writing well about food is a good appetite.

— A.J. Liebling

Makes 6 servings.
Per Serving: 336 Calories; 24g Fat (64.6% calories from fat); 14g Protein; 16g Carbohydrate; 1g Dietary Fiber; 165mg Cholesterol; 493mg Sodium.

Rice shaped pasta cooks quickly for a fast dinner.

Tuna Orzo

Serve hot, or cold with the cherry tomatoes as a traveling picnic. Allowing the flavors to marry before serving gives this pasta dish upscale flavor and taste.

2	cups orzo
1	small red onion – cut in 1/2 inch dice
8	ounces black olives – sliced
12	ounces tuna in water – drained
1	Tablespoon Italian seasoning
1/4	cup extra virgin olive oil
1/4	cup lemon juice – fresh
1	teaspoon dry mustard
1	teaspoon dill weed
1/2	cup white wine – or vegetable broth
1	pint cherry tomatoes
1	cup fresh Italian parsley – chopped
	Pepper – to taste

1. Boil water in a large pasta pot. Add orzo and cook according to package directions.
2. In a large sauté pan, sauté the onion, olives, tuna, and Italian herb seasoning in the olive oil and lemon juice for 3 minutes. Add the mustard, dill, and white wine and cook for 5 to 8 minutes. Stir often to make a creamy sauce with the tuna-mustard-wine base.
3. Add orzo to the tuna sauce. Heat for 1 minute until the mixture is well blended and warm throughout. Remove from heat and add cherry tomatoes. Garnish with parsley and season with pepper to taste.

Makes 6 servings.
Per Serving: 440 Calories; 15g Fat (30.9% calories from fat); 23g Protein; 51g Carbohydrate; 4g Dietary Fiber; 17mg Cholesterol; 538mg Sodium.

A rosy harmony of colors

Salmon with Texas Red and Peppercorn Pink

In France, red grapefruit is prized among the summer bounty.

Saffron rice is our favorite side dish with the salmon.

- 2 teaspoons rice vinegar
- 2 teaspoons soy sauce
- 1 Tablespoon pink peppercorns
- 2 teaspoons fresh ginger – grated
- 1 clove garlic – minced
- 1/4 teaspoon salt
- 1/4 teaspoon cayenne
- 1/4 cup olive oil
- 2 pounds salmon fillets – cut in 5 ounce portions
- Salt and pepper
- 2 Tablespoons olive oil
- 2 Texas Ruby Red grapefruits – peeled and sectioned
- 1 lemon – peeled and sectioned
- 1 lime – peeled and sectioned
- 1/4 cup cilantro leaves, whole

1. Prepare grill using a non-stick spray. Light and allow to pre-heat.
2. In a medium bowl, stir together the vinegar, soy sauce, peppercorns, ginger, garlic salt and cayenne until well blended. Whisk in 1/4 cup oil in a steady stream. Set aside.
3. Sprinkle the salmon fillets with salt and pepper, and brush with the two tablespoons of olive oil. Grill salmon over hot coals. Place fish meat side down for about three minutes on the freshly greased grill. Using a large spatula, turn fish to the skin side down to complete cooking. This should take about ten minutes total per inch of fish thickness.
4. Stir the fruit and cilantro into the mixture after the fish comes off the grill. Spoon over each filet and serve.

Makes 6 servings.
Per Serving: 312 Calories; 19g Fat (54.3% calories from fat); 31g Protein; 5g Carbohydrate; 1g Dietary Fiber; 79mg Cholesterol; 306mg Sodium.

Mediterranean in a Snap

1 1/2	pounds red snapper
2	Tablespoons vegetable oil
1	cup onion – cut in 1/4 inch dice
2	cloves garlic – minced
4	large tomatoes – seeded and diced
1 1/2	ounces raisins – 1 single serving box
1/4	cup pine nuts – toasted
6	kalamata olives – pitted and chopped
1/4	cup oregano leaves – fresh

1. Preheat oven to 350F.
2. Rinse fish and arrange in one layer in a large baking dish. Cook fish in preheated oven for approximately 5 minutes. Remove from oven and discard collected juices.
3. Heat oil in a large skillet. Sauté onions and garlic until onions are translucent. Add tomatoes, raisins, nuts and olives. Toss and sauté for 5 minutes more.
4. Cover fish with fresh oregano leaves. Pour hot tomato mixture gently over the fish and return to the oven for another 6–10 minutes. Serve while hot.

Tomatoes and oregano make it Italian; wine and tarragon make it French. Sour cream makes it Russian; lemon and cinnamon make it Greek. Soy sauce makes it Chinese; garlic makes it good.

— Alice May Brock

Makes 6 servings.
Per Serving: 246 Calories; 10g Fat (37.2% calories from fat); 26g Protein; 13g Carbohydrate; 2g Dietary Fiber; 42mg Cholesterol; 142mg Sodium.

Poisson à l'Orange

1 1/2 pounds cod fillet – or whitefish
1/2 small red onion – thinly sliced
1/2 cup orange juice
1/4 cup vegetable oil
2 Tablespoons orange zest
1 clove garlic
1 teaspoon Dijon mustard
1/2 teaspoon cumin
1/4 teaspoon celery salt
1/4 teaspoon salt
2 oranges – peeled and sectioned
1 red bell pepper – cut in 1/4 inch strips
1/3 cup green onion – sliced, (green and white)

1. Preheat oven to 350F.
2. Separate sliced onion rings and layer over the bottom of a large ceramic or glass dish. Rinse fish and pat dry. Lay skin side down in one layer on top of the onion rings. Refrigerate while preparing marinade.
3. In a non-reactive bowl, mix together the orange juice, oil, zest, garlic, mustard, cumin, celery salt and salt. Pour over the fish. Cover the dish with plastic wrap and return to refrigerator. Allow to marinate for at least 20 minutes, but no more than 30.
4. While fish is marinating, prepare the oranges, bell pepper, and green onion in a medium bowl. Stir lightly to combine. Cover with plastic wrap and store in refrigerator.
5. Remove the fish from the refrigerator and bake in the oven for 20 minutes. The fish will still be fleshy at the end of this baking time. Pour the orange mixture evenly over the fish and return to the oven for the remaining 5–10 minutes of baking time. [Note: Times will vary according to thickness of fish]
6. Remove fish from the pan and place on a platter to serve.

You don't have to have a snootful of arcane food knowledge to be a gourmet, that is. Why can't a gourmet be just some ordinary Joe or Jane who likes good grub, who can cook bacon without curling it, maybe, or who knows a good hamburger from a bad shrimp? Why can't we all be gourmets, and proud of it – confident, hungry, and to hell with the garnish?

— **Gourmet with a Garnish** by Colman Andrews, executive editor of *Saveur*

Makes 6 servings.
Per Serving: 220 Calories; 10g Fat (41.3% calories from fat); 21g Protein; 11g Carbohydrate; 2g Dietary Fiber; 49mg Cholesterol; 229mg Sodium.

Delicate lemongrass flavor highlights a mild fish such as tilapia.

Lemongrass Fish

- 3 cups water
- 1 cup white wine
- 2 Tablespoons fresh tarragon
- 1 teaspoon salt
- 1/2 teaspoon white pepper
- 1 celery rib – cut in 3 inch pieces
- 12 leek strips – (green only)
- 12 pieces lemongrass – cut in 3 inch pieces
- 1 1/2 pounds sea bass fillet – or tilapia
- 2 Tablespoons leek – finely chopped (white only)
- 1 Tablespoon butter

1. Bring water, wine, tarragon, salt, pepper, and celery to a boil in a large pot or fish poacher. Reduce heat to a simmer for about 10 minutes.
2. Lay rinsed fish out on a tray. Gently split each filet lengthwise down the center. Place two lemon grass pieces on one half and cover with the other half.
3. Dip the leek strips into the boiling water and remove when pliable. Using two strips per fish, gently tie each fish to secure the lemongrass inside.
4. Using a large spatula, lower the fish into the hot liquid. Simmer covered for about 5 minutes, then remove cover for remaining poaching time. Anticipate 7–10 minutes total for a one-inch thick fish fold-over combination.
5. Using the large spatula, carefully remove fish from the liquid and place on each plate. Turn the fish over so the tie is on the underside.
6. Place chopped white leek in a small bowl. Add 1/4 cup of the flavorful poaching liquid to the bowl. Quickly whisk in the butter to create a sauce and spoon over each fish.

"Love proves itself by deeds, so how am I to show my love? Great deeds are forbidden me. The only way I can prove my love is by scattering flowers and these flowers are every little sacrifice, every glance and word, and the doing of the least actions for love."

— St. Thérèse of Lisieux

Makes 6 servings.
Per Serving: 289 Calories; 5g Fat (15.8% calories from fat); 24g Protein; 35g Carbohydrate; trace Dietary Fiber; 52mg Cholesterol; 472mg Sodium.

As much recipes for living as formulae for cooking, cookbooks are forums for discussing the conduct of life, even the most pragmatic. Living within the constraints of their respective eras, they have used these texts to examine and shape their own and others' lives. Women found them useful points of departure for reflection.

— **Eat My Words**
by Janet Theophano

Shreveport Gumbo

2	Tablespoons all-purpose flour
2	Tablespoons oil
1	cup onions – cut in 1/2 inch dice
1/2	cup green onions – cut in 1/2 inch slices (white and green)
1/2	cup green bell pepper – cut in 1/2 inch dice
1/4	cup celery – cut in 1/2 inch dice
2	garlic cloves – minced
3	cups chicken broth
1 1/2	cups vegetable juice cocktail – spicy hot
1/2	teaspoon cayenne pepper
1/4	teaspoon thyme – crushed
2	bay leaves
28	ounces canned tomatoes
10	ounces frozen okra – cut into 1/2 inch rounds
1 1/2	pounds shrimp – shelled & deveined
2	cups chicken thighs without skin – cooked & cubed
4	cups cooked white rice

1. In a large Dutch oven, combine flour and oil to make a roux. Stir constantly for about 20–35 minutes to prevent burning.
2. Remove from heat and immediately add onions, peppers, celery and garlic until roux quits bubbling. Cook over low heat for 10 minutes, stirring constantly. Slowly pour in chicken broth and vegetable juice.
3. Stir in dried spices, tomatoes and okra. Bring to a boil. Reduce heat, cover and simmer for an hour. Stir occasionally.
4. Remove bay leaves. Add shrimp and chicken and stir. Cook until shrimp are light pink. Serve in a warm bowl over 1/2 cup rice.

Makes 8 servings.
Per Serving: 354 Calories; 7g Fat (18.7% calories from fat); 31g Protein; 40g Carbohydrate; 3g Dietary Fiber; 157mg Cholesterol; 719mg Sodium.

For a dinner party, prepare everything ahead and gather the guests to grill the fish with a flourish.

Speckled Blue Marlin on the Thai High Seas

1 1/2	pounds Blue Marlin
3	cups water
2	chicken bouillon cubes – crushed
1/2	cup brown rice
1/2	cup wild rice
2	cups Bok choy — 1/2 inch dice, white
1	Tablespoon fresh ginger – peeled and minced
1	teaspoon salt
1	teaspoon sugar
1	Tablespoon cream sherry
2	Tablespoons vegetable oil
1	Tablespoon Teriyaki sauce
1	teaspoon rice vinegar
6	Tablespoons sesame seeds
3/4	teaspoon ginger

1. Preheat grill. Rinse fish and slice into 4 ounce portions. (This is approximately palm size) Return to refrigerator until ready to grill.
2. Pour 3 cups water and chicken bouillon cubes in large saucepan. Bring to a boil, and add rices. Cover and simmer for 45 minutes.
3. Cut and remove the green leaves from the Bok Choy. Chop the remaining white stalk into 1/2 inch dice.
4. Place measured salt and sugar into a tiny glass bowl. Pour measured cream sherry in a separate small bowl to prepare for stir-fry cooking.
5. Heat oil until lightly smoking in wok skillet, or large frypan. Toss in Bok Choy and sauté quickly about 3 minutes until juices start to gather. Add ginger and continue to stir fry for another minute. Add sugar/salt mixture and distribute thoroughly. Add cream sherry last, stir fry for about 30 seconds to 1 minute and remove from heat. Keep warm while finishing recipe preparation.

Substitutions for fish can include swordfish, and fresh tuna.

6. Mix teriyaki sauce and rice vinegar in a large glass dish that will hold the fish in one layer. Marinate each side, turning after 3–4 minutes on each large side. ***DO NOT*** marinate longer, because the vinegar will 'cook' the fish. If necessary, remove fish to a separate plate if not ready to grill.
7. Tap approximately 1/8 teaspoon (2 dashes) of powdered ginger on top of each piece of fish.
8. When rice has approximately 10 minutes remaining, prepare to grill fish. Place each piece on the grill and cook for 6+3 minutes per inch.

   [This translates to: A 1 inch thick piece rests 6 minutes on the first side, and half the amount of time (3 minutes) on the other. Increase or decrease this time with the varying thickness.] Sprinkle 1 Tablespoon sesame seeds on Marlin, turning to distribute on all sides.

9. To serve, place a ring of approximately 1/2 cup wild rice pilaf on the plate. Place about 3 Tablespoons of Bok Choy mixture in the center. Put fish on top of the sautéed Bok Choy. Serve while fish is still steaming from the grill.

The most time saving elements in your kitchen are skill and a good knife.

Makes 6 servings.
Per Serving: 351 Calories; 14g Fat (37.2% calories from fat); 28g Protein; 27g Carbohydrate; 2g Dietary Fiber; 44mg Cholesterol; 842mg Sodium.

Luscious Linguini with Arugula and Oven-Roasted Tomatoes

2 pints cherry tomatoes — oven-roasted
2 cups arugula leaves — about 10 ounces
1 pound whole wheat pasta — linguine or fettucine
2 Tablespoons extra virgin olive oil
2 Tablespoons butter
2 Tablespoons lemon zest
1 cup heavy cream — room temperature
1/4 cup Parmesan cheese — grated
Salt and freshly ground black pepper — to taste

1. Slice cherry tomatoes in half and bake in 200F oven for about four to five hours, or place in a warming drawer overnight.
2. Place the roasted tomatoes and the arugula leaves into a medium serving bowl.
3. Cook the pasta according to package directions. Drain and toss with the two Tablespoons of oil to coat. Set aside.
4. Melt butter in a three-quart saucepan. Add the lemon zest, and sauté for one minute. Stir in the heavy cream, and heat thoroughly. Do Not Boil.
5. Add the Parmesan cheese, and whisk rapidly until smooth. Season with salt, and freshly ground pepper.
6. Add cooked linguine to the pot with the cream mixture, and toss until well coated.
7. Pour warmed pasta into the serving bowl over tomatoes and arugula. Toss to wilt the arugula. Serve immediately with additional grated Parmesan.

The purpose of a cookery book is one and unmistakable. Its object can conceivably be no other than to increase the happiness of mankind.

— Recipe for Morality by Joseph Conrad

Makes 6 servings.
Per Serving: 513 Calories; 25g Fat (42.4% calories from fat); 14g Protein; 63g Carbohydrate; 8g Dietary Fiber; 67mg Cholesterol; 133mg Sodium.

So impressed by the dinner served in this city on the edge of the Abruzzo National Park, I asked the chef of Poppeoli Jore for his recipe.

Pasta Pescasseroli

- 2 Tablespoons unsalted butter
- 2 Tablespoons extra virgin olive oil
- 1 cup onion – cut in 1/2 inch dice
- 2 cloves garlic – minced
- 6 large pepperoncini peppers – cut in 1/2 inch pieces
- 1 bay leaf
- 1 Tablespoon dried oregano
- 6 ounces pancetta – cut in 1/4 inch dice
- 1 cup white wine
- 2 vegetable bouillon cubes – crushed
- 6 ounces porcini mushrooms – cut in 1/2 inch dice
- 3 large tomatoes – seeded and cut in 1/2 inch dice
- 1 pound fettucine – or guitar string pasta
- 1 Tablespoon extra virgin olive oil
- 1/4 cup fresh basil leaves – torn

1. In a large skillet, melt the butter over medium heat. Add olive oil.
2. Sauté onion and garlic until the onion is translucent. Add pepperoncini, bay leaf, oregano and pancetta. Stir to combine. Add white wine and bring to a boil.
3. Stir in porcini mushrooms and tomatoes. Reduce heat to simmer for 40 minutes, stirring occasionally.
4. Prepare pasta according to package directions. Drain. Place in a large bowl and toss with one Tablespoon olive oil.
5. Sprinkle fresh basil over the pasta. Pour hot porcini mixture over the pasta and serve.

Makes 8 servings.
Per Serving: 430 Calories; 11g Fat (23.9% calories from fat); 16g Protein; 64g Carbohydrate; 5g Dietary Fiber; 23mg Cholesterol; 746mg Sodium.

Goat cheese varieties are plentiful – try many!

Whole Wheat Pasta with Goat Cheese, Walnuts, and Sun-Dried Tomatoes

When my pediatrician discovered my two year old loved this at dinner, he swore he would never ask if he was a finicky eater again.

12 ounces whole-wheat pasta – linguine or fettucine
1/2 cup extra virgin olive oil
1 Tablespoon garlic – minced
5 ounces goat cheese – Montrachet
1/2 cup walnuts – toasted
1/4 cup sun-dried tomatoes – slivered
1 Tablespoon mint leaves – finely chopped
1 Tablespoon basil leaves – finely chopped
1 Tablespoon fresh oregano – finely chopped
1 Tablespoon rosemary sprigs – finely chopped
Salt and pepper – to taste
1/2 cup Parmesan cheese – grated

1. Bring a large pot of 4 quarts of water to a boil. Cook the pasta according to the package directions. Drain well.
2. Heat the olive oil in a large skillet and sauté the garlic over low heat for 1 minute. Toss the cooked pasta in the oil to coat.
3. Hold back one ounce of the goat cheese for garnish. Crumble the remaining goat cheese over the pasta and stir to coat with the warm oil. Add the walnuts, sun-dried tomatoes, and fresh herbs. Mix the ingredients thoroughly. Season with salt and pepper, as needed.
4. Remove from heat and pour onto a large platter. Top with the remaining goat cheese and the Parmesan cheese. Serve.

Makes 8 servings.
Per Serving: 425 Calories; 26g Fat (53.9% calories from fat); 16g Protein; 35g Carbohydrate; 4g Dietary Fiber; 23mg Cholesterol; 191mg Sodium.

Spicy Italian Red Sauce

Enough sauce for two pounds of spaghetti, or one pound of pasta and sauce for lasagna later.

1	pound Italian sausage – spicy
1	pound lean ground beef
1	bell pepper – cut in 1/2 inch dice
1	large onion – cut in 1/2 inch dice
2	garlic cloves – minced
36 1/2	ounces tomatoes, canned
30	ounces tomato sauce
6	ounces tomato paste
2	Tablespoons dried oregano
1	Tablespoon dried basil
1	Tablespoon dried rosemary
1	Tablespoon dried sage
2	teaspoons dried thyme
2	teaspoons dried chervil
2	teaspoons black pepper
1	teaspoon salt

1. Crumble sausage and ground beef into large Dutch oven. Brown meat. Drain fat and return to pan.
2. Add bell pepper, onion, and garlic. Stir frequently. Cook until tender, about 5 to 7 minutes.
3. Add tomatoes, sauce, paste and all dried spices. Stir to combine. Simmer, covered, over low heat for about an hour.

Makes 12 servings.
Per Serving: 293 Calories; 20g Fat (60.5% calories from fat); 15g Protein; 15g Carbohydrate; 4g Dietary Fiber; 57mg Cholesterol; 1150mg Sodium.

"Tis an ill cook that cannot lick his own fingers"
Romeo and Juliet, Act IV Scene ii

Spicy Sesame Pasta

1 1/2 pounds skinless chicken breast halves
4 green onions — cleaned and halved
4 sprigs cilantro
1/4 teaspoon salt
1/4 teaspoon pepper
1/4 cup hoisin sauce

1 pound fettucine — or linguine
dash salt
2 Tablespoons vegetable oil

1/3 cup peanut butter, chunky
1/2 cup soy sauce, low sodium
4 garlic cloves — minced
3 Tablespoons fresh ginger — minced
1 Tablespoon rice wine vinegar
1 Tablespoon brown sugar
1 teaspoon Chinese five spice
1 teaspoon red pepper flakes
2 Tablespoons sesame oil
1 Tablespoon chile pepper oil — or to taste
1 Tablespoon vegetable oil

2 cups snow peas — trimmed, (8 ounces)
2 cups bean sprouts — (8 ounces)
1 can baby corn — drained and rinsed
1 red bell pepper — cut in 1/2 inch dice
1 cup jicama — cut in 2 inch x 1/2 inch strips
1/2 cup cilantro — chopped
4 green onions — cut in 1/2 inch pieces

Garnish
1 Tablespoon lemon juice
3 Tablespoons sesame seeds

I love to take this in the picnic cooler when I attend Shakespeare in the Park. It is my favorite summer date in Dallas. www.shakespearedallas.org

1. Place the chicken in a Dutch oven and cover with water. Bring to a boil and skim the foam from the top. Add the green onions, cilantro, salt and pepper. Cover and reduce the heat. Simmer for 30 minutes or until the chicken is tender. Remove from heat, drain, and let stand to cool.
2. Cook the pasta in boiling, salted water according to package directions in a large pasta pot. Do not drain water. Remove pasta into large bowl and toss with 2 tablespoons vegetable oil.
3. Return the pasta water to a boil. Prepare a bowl of ice water. Using the inner liner of the pasta pot, or an immersible colander, plunge the cleaned snow peas into the boiling water for 30 seconds. They should be a bright green color and still crisp. Immediately pour peas into the ice water to stop the cooking. Drain and add to the pasta bowl. Repeat the process with the fresh bean sprouts by plunging them for 20 seconds, then transferring them into the ice water. Drain and add to the pasta bowl.
4. Combine the peanut butter and soy sauce in a food processor workbowl. Stir with a spatula to combine. Add garlic, ginger, vinegar, brown sugar, five-spice powder, and pepper flakes. Start processor. With the motor running, add oils through the feed tube and thoroughly combine. Set aside.
5. Remove the cooled chicken from the bone. Cut into bite size pieces, and toss with the hoisin sauce. Add to the pasta bowl.
6. Add the baby corn, red bell pepper, jicama, cilantro and scallions to the pasta bowl.
7. Pour sauce over the pasta mixture and toss well to combine. Refrigerate until ready to serve.
8. Pour the pasta mixture onto a serving platter. Sprinkle lemon juice lightly over the pasta to freshen it. Garnish with the sesame seeds in a pattern over the pasta for a beautiful presentation.

Makes 8 servings.
Per Serving: 527 Calories; 18g Fat (30.4% calories from fat); 30g Protein; 62g Carbohydrate; 6g Dietary Fiber; 40mg Cholesterol; 911mg Sodium.

Ginger-Garlic Pasta

1 pound angel hair pasta
3 Tablespoons unsalted butter
1/2 cup olive oil
1 cup carrot – cut in 1/4 inch dice
1/2 cup white wine – or chicken broth
2 Tablespoons fresh ginger – finely cut, not minced
1 Tablespoon garlic – finely cut, not minced
1 teaspoon dried oregano
1/2 teaspoon salt
1/2 teaspoon hot red pepper flakes
1 cup water
2 Tablespoons green onion – sliced, green and white
1/2 cup Parmesan cheese – grated

Grilled chicken breasts go well with this pasta

1. Prepare pasta according to package directions. Drain and toss with butter in a large serving bowl. Set aside.
2. Heat oil in a medium skillet and sauté the carrot for three minutes.
3. Gently pour in the wine and stir. Add the ginger, garlic, oregano, salt, and pepper flakes. Cook for five minutes.
4. Add one cup of water (or additional broth), bring to a boil, and cook for five minutes uncovered.
5. Pour the sauce over the angel hair and toss to combine. Sprinkle with scallions. Serve with freshly grated Parmesan cheese.

Makes 6 servings.
Per Serving: 549 Calories; 27g Fat (45.4% calories from fat); 13g Protein; 60g Carbohydrate; 3g Dietary Fiber; 21mg Cholesterol; 318mg Sodium.

Choose savory sage-based sausage or bold spicy hot sausage for variations

Italian Sausage and Penne

Other pasta choices, such as rigatoni, work well with this recipe.

- 1 Tablespoon olive oil
- 4 cloves garlic – slivered
- 1 pound Italian sausage – spicy or sweet
- 1 teaspoon salt
- 4 cups broccoli florets – cut in bite size pieces
- 12 ounces penne pasta
- 1 Tablespoon olive oil
- 1/2 teaspoon salt
- 1/4 cup Parmesan cheese – freshly grated
- 1/2 teaspoon fennel seeds
- Freshly ground pepper – to taste
- 3 Tablespoons fresh fennel ferns – optional

1. Heat 1 Tablespoon of oil in a large skillet. Add the garlic, and sauté over medium heat until it is golden and crisp, about 3 to 5 minutes. Remove the garlic with a slotted spoon to a large pasta bowl. Set it aside.
2. In the same skillet, crumble the sausage. Cook over medium heat until browned, about 3 to 4 minutes. Cover and simmer until cooked through, about 10 minutes. Remove the meat with a slotted spoon to the large pasta bowl. Set aside. Pour off all but 2 Tablespoons fat.
3. Bring a large pot of water to a boil. Stir in salt and add the broccoli. Blanch for 3 minutes to reveal the rich green color. Remove the broccoli with a slotted spoon to the large pasta bowl. Reserve the cooking liquid.
4. Bring the broccoli cooking liquid to a boil again, and add the penne. Cook at a rolling boil according to package directions, until just tender. Measure 1/2 cup of the cooking liquid into the large saucepan. Drain pasta and place in a large serving bowl. Toss in 1 Tablespoon olive oil to coat. Keep warm.
5. Heat the sausage, broccoli and garlic with the reserved 1/2 cup cooking liquid. Add salt and stir to heat through.
6. Add the sausage mixture to the pasta. Top with the Parmesan, fennel seeds, pepper, and fennel ferns. Toss well, and serve immediately.

Makes 8 servings.
Per Serving: 409 Calories; 23g Fat (50.3% calories from fat); 16g Protein; 35g Carbohydrate; 2g Dietary Fiber; 45mg Cholesterol; 874mg Sodium.

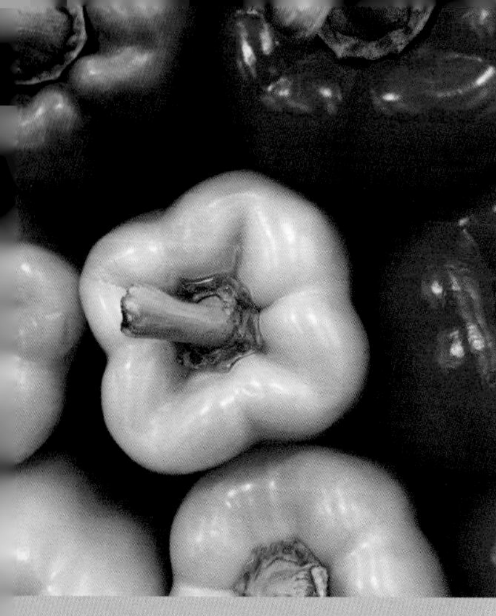

Pork Chop Towers

1 1/2	pounds pork chops – boneless
1	Tablespoon marjoram
1	small red onion – thinly sliced
20	ounces diced tomatoes with spices – undrained
2	large bell peppers
1	cup carrot – cut in 1/2 inch dice
1	cup instant brown rice
12	Kalamata olives – pitted and chopped

1. Preheat oven to 350F.
2. Rinse pork chops and pat dry. Place in one layer in a baking dish. Sprinkle chops with marjoram.
3. Layer thinly sliced onions on top of each pork chop. Dice remaining onion, if any, and place in a large bowl.
4. Slice the bottom and top from each bell pepper; remove seeds and large veins. Cut into 1 inch rings. Place one on each chop. Dice remaining bell pepper, and add to the large bowl.
5. Add one Tablespoon carrots into each pepper ring. Add remaining carrots to the large bowl. Add two Tablespoons of raw rice to each pepper ring.
6. Pour tomatoes with their liquid into the large bowl of vegetables. Stir coarsely chopped Kalamata olives into tomato sauce. Spoon tomato mixture on top of each chop. Spoon liquid from the bowl into each ring to cook the rice. Stir in additional rice (if any) and pour the remainder of the tomato sauce into the baking dish.
7. Bake for 30–35 minutes.

A fellow volunteer for the 1984 Republican Convention in Dallas shared this recipe with me while we were working a registration table. I think of her fondly each time I prepare this dish.

Makes 6 servings.
Per Serving: 423 Calories; 21g Fat (44.7% calories from fat); 32g Protein; 26g Carbohydrate; 3g Dietary Fiber; 93mg Cholesterol; 210mg Sodium.

Tasty slivers of garlic remain in the sliced lamb when served

When we lived in France, spring lamb that grazed on wild sage made this a tender dish. A good quality lamb from Australia is also delicious.

Garlic Roasted Leg of Lamb

8 pounds leg of lamb
5 cloves garlic — slivered
2 Tablespoons olive oil
1/4 cup Herbs de Provence
2 large leeks
1 head garlic

1. Preheat oven to 425F. Using a non-stick spray, prepare a shallow roasting pan.
2. Trim the lamb of excess fat. Using a small sharp knife, make several, evenly distributed cuts in the lamb and slide the garlic slivers completely into the meat. Drizzle the oil over the lamb and rub into the meat with your hands.
3. Remove the tops of the leeks, and about 1 inch of the green ends. Slice lengthwise, fan open under running water, and clean of any sandy residue. Cut to separate the green and white sections. Place the green part from the leek flat on the roasting rack. Place lamb on top of the green of the leek. Sprinkle Herbs de Provence over the lamb and press gently to adhere.
4. Separate the remaining cloves from the head of garlic, leaving paper skins intact. Nestle along the base of the lamb. Slice white portion of the leek and sprinkle over the garlic cloves.
5. Place the pan in the center of the oven, and roast for 45 minutes. Reduce the heat to 375F and continue roasting for about an hour and 15 minutes or until the internal temperature of the lamb reaches 140F on an instant-read thermometer. Remove from the oven.
6. Allow lamb to rest for 15 minutes before carving. The temperature will rise to 145F for medium-rare after the meat rests. Sliced leeks and roasted garlic can be used for a sauce if desired, or otherwise discarded.

Makes 10 servings.
Per Serving: 697 Calories; 52g Fat (68.0% calories from fat); 52g Protein; 3g Carbohydrate; trace Dietary Fiber; 198mg Cholesterol; 164mg Sodium.

Polynesian Pork Steaks

Yes, I really mean baby food. It has little sugar and minimal salt. I always have a use for those jars.

- 1 1/2 pounds pork shoulder — thinly sliced
- 1/2 teaspoon salt
- 1 tablespoon oil
- 8 ounces plums — baby food, 2 small jars
- 1/4 cup coconut flakes
- 1/4 cup water
- 1 Tablespoon vinegar — (or rice vinegar)
- 2 teaspoons low sodium soy sauce
- 1/2 teaspoon ginger
- 1 teaspoon lemon zest
- 3 ounces banana chips — dried

1. Trim and season steaks with salt. Heat oil in a large skillet over high heat. Brown the steaks on both sides.
2. Stir together remaining ingredients in a bowl and gently pour over steaks. Cover and reduce to simmer, Cook until tender, about 35 to 40 minutes.

What do babies dream of in their small little head?
What do they dream of when they are dried and gently fed?

What could babies dream of when their life's so full of ease?
Of standing on two feet? Or crawling on two knees?

Babies dream dreams, only sweet and pure
But their mothers dream of babies, of that I am sure.

— Kay Berry

Makes 6 servings.
Per Serving: 331 Calories; 24g Fat (63.6% calories from fat); 15g Protein; 15g Carbohydrate; 2g Dietary Fiber; 60mg Cholesterol; 309mg Sodium.

Lamb Salad with Sun-Dried Tomatoes and Rosemary

- 1 cup sun-dried tomato halves – cut in 1/4 inch slices
- 1/2 cup boiling water
- 2 cloves garlic – minced
- 1/2 cup fresh basil leaves – chiffonnade
- 1 Tablespoon fresh rosemary – minced
- 1/4 cup balsamic vinegar
- 1 Tablespoon black pepper
- 1/4 cup olive oil
- Salt – to taste
- 1 1/2 pounds lamb sirloin – roasted and cooled
- 10 ounces fresh spinach – washed and trimmed

The marinated lamb and a small quantity of the spinach can be put into a baguette for a delicious sandwich.

1. Place sundried tomatoes in boiling water bath, and soak for 20 minutes or until soft.
2. Combine the garlic, basil, rosemary, vinegar and pepper in a medium bowl. Whisk in the olive oil to emulsify.
3. Cut lamb in 1/4 inch wide slices. Add to bowl. Drain tomatoes and add to bowl. Stir to combine.
4. Let marinate for at least one hour. If not using within the hour, refrigerate. If refrigerating, let stand at room temperature one hour before serving.
5. Add salt to taste. Stir lamb and marinade just before serving. Drain dressing into a measuring cup and drizzle over spinach. Toss lightly to distribute. Divide evenly over 6 plates and top with lamb mixture. Serve.

Makes 6 servings.
Per Serving: 436 Calories; 30g Fat (58.5% calories from fat); 22g Protein; 25g Carbohydrate; 6g Dietary Fiber; 63mg Cholesterol; 914mg Sodium.

Onions can make even heirs and widows weep.
— Benjamin Franklin

Mexican Pot Roast

4	pounds roast, trimmed
	Salt and pepper
1	Tablespoon oil
1	cup onion – cut in 1/2 inch dice
1	clove garlic – minced
30	ounces kidney beans, canned
15 1/2	ounces tomatoes, canned
8	ounces green chiles
1	teaspoon salt
1/2	teaspoon oregano
1/2	teaspoon pepper
1/4	teaspoon red pepper flakes
3 1/2	ounces black olives – sliced

1. Preheat oven to 325F.
2. Season meat with salt and pepper. Heat oil over high heat in a Dutch oven. Brown quickly on all sides and remove to a plate.
3. Add onion and garlic to the pot and sauté until tender. Add all other ingredients except olives. Heat to boiling, then reduce heat to a simmer. Return meat to the pot, and submerge in the liquid. Top with olives.
4. Cover tightly; cook at 325F for about 3 hours until fork tender.

For the second appearance of this dish, dice the meat into bite size pieces. Prepare rotoni pasta and stir to combine for a stew.

Makes 10 servings.
Per Serving: 365 Calories; 12g Fat (29.2% calories from fat); 45g Protein; 18g Carbohydrate; 4g Dietary Fiber; 105mg Cholesterol; 765mg Sodium.

A kiss of wine with golden raisins

Pork Chops with Raisin-Pignolia Sauce

2	boneless pork top loin chops — 4 to 5 ounces each
1	teaspoon olive oil
1/4	cup shallots — sliced thin
1	teaspoon all-purpose flour
1/2	cup chicken broth
2	Tablespoons white wine
1/4	cup golden raisins
2	Tablespoons pignolia — toasted
1	teaspoon rosemary — chopped

1. Preheat broiler. Prepare broiling pan with nonstick cooking spray. Arrange chops on the pan and broil until nicely browned, about 4 to 5 minutes on each side.
2. While chops are broiling, prepare sauce. In a nonstick skillet heat olive oil over medium heat. Add shallots and cook until golden, about two minutes. Sprinkle with flour and stir quickly to combine. Stir in broth and wine. Bring mixture to a boil, then reduce heat to simmer. Stir in raisins, pignolia (pine nuts) and rosemary. Let flavors blend, about 3 to 4 minutes. Remove from heat.
3. To serve, arrange chops on serving platter and top with sauce.

Eating is not merely a material pleasure. Eating well gives a spectacular joy to life and contributes immensely to goodwill and happy companionship. It is of great importance to the morale.

— Elsa Schiaparelli, Italian-French designer

Makes 2 servings.
Per Serving: 302 Calories; 12g Fat (36.3% calories from fat); 25g Protein; 23g Carbohydrate; 1g Dietary Fiber; 51mg Cholesterol; 239mg Sodium.

Traditional Boeuf Bourguignon is marked by the signature small, round onions.

Boeuf Bourguignon

2 pounds beef chuck – cut in 1 inch cubes
1/4 cup all-purpose flour
2 Tablespoons vegetable oil
salt and pepper
1 1/2 cups onion – cut in 1/2 inch dice
4 slices bacon – cut in 1 inch pieces
2 large garlic cloves – sliced thin
1/2 cup carrot – cut in 1/2 inch dice
1 leek – cut in 1/2 inch slices
1/4 cup all-purpose flour
1/4 cup Cognac
1 teaspoon dried thyme
1 bay leaf
2 cups red wine – Burgundy
1/4 cup all-purpose flour
16 ounces mushrooms – sliced
16 ounces pearl onions
1/2 cup parsley sprigs

Some recipes call for flaming the cognac to burn off the alcohol. I prefer to simmer it into the dish.

This can be prepared over a low flame on the stove, or in the oven. The stove method saves a bit of cooking time while the oven version clears the counter and cooktop a little faster.

1. Coat the beef cubes with flour. Heat oil in a large skillet. Brown the beef in at least four batches, to retain the heat of the oil. Overcrowding the beef in the pan will make it steam and turn grey instead of sear in the flavor. Remove the meat with a slotted spoon to a 4 quart covered baking dish. Preheat oven to 350F.
2. Add the chopped onions, bacon, garlic, carrots, and leek slices to the skillet. Stir continuously until the onions begin to caramelize and brown. Sprinkle the additional flour over the mixture to thicken the sauce. Add Cognac and stir to combine. Simmer gently for 3 to 5 minutes.
3. Sprinkle dried thyme over beef. Pour the onion vegetable mixture over the beef and slide the bay leaf alongside. Pour in the Burgundy wine and add just enough water to cover the meat. Cover with a lid and bake for 1 1/2 hours.
4. Remove 1/2 cup of hot broth from the casserole. Stir 1/4 cup flour into the broth and return to the pot. Stir all the contents and return casserole to the oven. Bake for 2 more hours.
5. After taking the casserole from the oven, turn oven off. Remove the meat to a platter with a slotted spoon. Strain the cooked vegetables from the broth and discard solids. Return broth and meat to the casserole dish. Do not cover. Return casserole to the off, but still warm oven.
6. Melt butter in the skillet. Add mushrooms and sauté until lightly browned. Add the small onions. Cover and cook until the onions are tender. Add the mushrooms and onions to the casserole dish. Stir to combine. Garnish with parsley.

Makes 8 servings.
Per Serving: 440 Calories; 23g Fat (56.7% calories from fat); 23g Protein; 22g Carbohydrate; 3g Dietary Fiber; 68mg Cholesterol; 292mg Sodium.

Found often at our table when we had guests in Paris.

Tenderloin de Porc Rôti

- 2 1/2 pounds pork tenderloin – rinsed
- 1 cup apple cider
- 5 ounces dried apples – cut in 1/2 inch pieces
- 4 large carrots – cut in 1 inch pieces
- 2 large onions – cut in 1 inch pieces
- 15 ounces chicken broth
- 1 Tablespoon chervil
- 2 teaspoons thyme
- 1 teaspoon ground cardamom
- 1 teaspoon black pepper
- 1/2 teaspoon salt
- 1/4 teaspoon anise seed
- 3 cloves garlic – minced
- 1 cup apple cider
- 2 Tablespoons butter

1. Preheat oven to 350F. Pour cider into a small bowl. Add dried apples and let stand while preparing other ingredients.
2. Using a non-stick spray, prepare a roasting pan for the tenderloin. Place the onion and carrot mixture in the bottom of the pan and pour the apple and cider mixture over it. Add the chicken broth and stir to combine.
3. Combine all dried spices in a small glass dish. Stirring with a spoon, add the minced garlic. Pour spice mixture onto a sheet of waxed paper, and roll tenderloin in the spices to completely cover. Gently lift spiced tenderloin and place on the rack of vegetables.
4. Place roasting pan in the oven. After 30 minutes, baste the loin evenly with the pan juices. Set the timer for 35 minutes per pound. During the last 15 minutes of cooking time, add the additional cup of apple cider to the broth, and baste again. Cook until the loin reaches 150F–160F.
5. When the roasting is complete, remove the loin from the pan and allow to rest for 10–15 minutes before carving. Remove the vegetables with a slotted spoon and discard. Whisk 2 tablespoons of butter into the pan juices and heat to a simmer.

I frequently create a vegetable 'rack' to roast meats. This adds flavor without a lot of labor.

Sliced roast on a large platter is beautifully served with about 1/2 cup of the pan juices. Serve the rest of the juice in a small gravy pitcher.

WHAT NOW?

Can't find apple cider? Add 2 Tablespoons apple cider vinegar to 1 cup pure apple juice. The sweet and tart combination will substitute easily.

Makes 8 servings.
Per Serving: 307 Calories; 8g Fat (24.3% calories from fat); 32g Protein; 26g Carbohydrate; 4g Dietary Fiber; 100mg Cholesterol; 434mg Sodium.

If doubling the recipe, only prepare a 4 egg quantity at a time. The frittata will not cook through or puff up if the quantity in the pan is too large.

Summer Spinach Fritatta

- 3/4 cup onion – cut in 1/2 inch dice
- 2 cloves garlic – minced
- 1 Tablespoon unsalted butter
- 4 eggs
- 1 1/2 teaspoons Herbes de Provence – or 1 T fresh thyme
- 1/2 teaspoon salt
- 1/2 teaspoon pepper – freshly ground
- 3 cups chopped spinach – about 5 ounces fresh
- 1 Tablespoon cream sherry
- 1 Tablespoon sesame seeds

1. Using a 10-inch pan with a heat-proof handle, melt butter and sauté onion and garlic until onions are golden.
2. Lightly beat eggs in a medium bowl. Add herbs, salt and pepper. Stir into onion and garlic mixture.
3. Preheat broiler.
4. Sauté spinach in the pan until just wilted. Stir in sherry and mix to combine. Spread spinach across pan in an even layer.
5. Gently pour egg mixture over the spinach. Using a heat treated spatula, gently prod the center of the frittata to move uncooked egg to the bottom of the pan. While mixture is still wet on the top, slip pan into broiler. ***DO NOT*** leave broiler unattended! After 1–2 minutes, the egg mixture will begin to puff up. When the center appears firm, remove from oven and sprinkle with sesame seeds
6. Cut into 4 wedge pieces and serve immediately.

Makes 4 servings.
Per Serving: 132 Calories; 9g Fat (61.6% calories from fat); 8g Protein; 5g Carbohydrate; 2g Dietary Fiber; 220mg Cholesterol; 356mg Sodium.

Chayotes are a pear shaped squash which have been cultivated since pre-Columbian times and are plentiful in southern Mexico.

Grilled Chayote Relleno

- 6 chayote squash
- 2 Tablespoons vegetable oil
- 1 onion – cut in 1/2 inch dice
- 8 ounces mushrooms – cut in 1/2 inch dice
- 2 garlic cloves – minced
- 1 poblano pepper – seeded, cut in 1/4 inch dice
- 1 teaspoon ground cumin
- 2 tomatoes – seeded, chopped
- 1 teaspoon oregano
- 1/4 cup cilantro – chopped
- 2 tablespoons toasted almonds – chopped
- 1/4 cup lime juice
- 1/2 cup queso fresco – grated

1. Preheat oven to 350F. Prepare a large pot of water to boil.
2. Plunge chayote into the pot of boiling water for 20 minutes. Remove from water, pat dry and allow to cool slightly. Cut chayote in half and remove the large seed and coarse fiber.
3. Prepare a grill with non-stick spray. Grill squash until tender, about 10 minutes. Cool slightly. Scoop out most of flesh, leaving 1/4 inch thick shell. Season shell with salt and pepper. Chop chayote flesh into 1/2 inch pieces. Set aside.
4. Heat oil in a large heavy skillet over medium high heat. Add onion and sauté until tender, about 5 minutes. Add mushrooms and cook until most of liquid evaporates.
5. Add garlic, poblano and cumin and sauté until fragrant. Add tomatoes. Stir until most of liquid evaporates. Stir in reserved chayote flesh, oregano, cilantro, and almonds. Remove from heat and stir in the lime juice. Season to taste with salt and pepper.
6. Spoon mixture into shells. Sprinkle with cheese. Arrange shells in large baking pan. Bake until heated through and the cheese melts, about 10 minutes.

Makes 6 servings.
Per Serving: 145 Calories; 9g Fat (48.8% calories from fat); 5g Protein; 17g Carbohydrate; 3g Dietary Fiber; 3mg Cholesterol; 22mg Sodium.

3 cups of all-purpose flour can be used, however, you lose the fiber advantage. Roll the dough a little large and lay string cheese along the rim of the crust. Fold the edge over to make a cheese stuffed crust.

Pizza Pleasin' Dough

- 1 cup whole-wheat flour
- 2 cups all-purpose flour
- 1 package yeast – fast-acting
- 1 Tablespoon honey
- 2 Tablespoons olive oil
- 1 teaspoon salt
- 1 cup water – hot (150F)

1. Combine the flour and yeast in the standing mixer workbowl, and toss gently with a fork to distribute the yeast. Secure the paddle attachment in the mixer (not the dough hook).
2. Combine the honey, olive oil and salt into the mixture. Turn the mixer on a low speed, and gently pour the hot water into the flour. Increase the speed and mix until the dough pulls easily from the sides of the bowl and a ball of dough is formed.
3. If required, knead on a floured surface until a smooth consistency. Place in a greased bowl, and let rise in a warm place until doubled in size or about 15–20 minutes.
4. Punch down dough and let rest for five minutes, or cover and refrigerate for up to three hours.
5. For an extra large pizza, or a large pizza with thick crust, roll the mixture out to the desired size round. For two pizzas, divide the dough in half and roll out to a thin crust.

Makes 8 servings.
Per Serving: 205 Calories; 4g Fat (17.4% calories from fat); 6g Protein; 37g Carbohydrate; 3g Dietary Fiber; 0mg Cholesterol; 269mg Sodium.

Smoked Gouda Polenta with Dancing Skirt Tomatoes

Rounding Out The Plate

Confetti Risotto

- 5 cups chicken broth
- 3 Tablespoons unsalted butter
- 1 Tablespoon extra virgin olive oil
- 1/2 cup onion – cut in 1/4 inch pieces
- 1/2 cup celery – cut in 1/4 inch pieces
- 1 1/2 cups arborio rice
- 1/2 cup dry white wine
- 1 red bell pepper – cut in 1/2 inch pieces
- 1/3 cup Parmesan cheese – grated
- 2 Tablespoons fresh thyme
- Salt – to taste

1. In a medium saucepan, bring the chicken stock to a simmer. Meanwhile, heat the butter and oil in a heavy 4-quart casserole over medium heat. Add the onion and celery. Sauté for one to two minutes, until they begin to soften; do not brown.
2. Add the rice, and stir for one minute, making sure all the grains are well coated. Add the wine, and stir until it is completely absorbed. Add the simmering chicken stock, 1/2 cup at a time, stirring frequently. Wait until each addition is almost completely absorbed before adding the next 1/2 cup. Reserve about 1/4 cup to add at the end. Stir frequently to prevent sticking.
3. After 20 to 25 minutes, when the rice is tender, but still firm, stir in the red bell pepper. Add the reserved 1/4 cup of stock. Turn off the heat, and immediately add the thyme and the Parmesan cheese. Stir vigorously to combine with the rice. Season with salt, and allow to cool.

If preparing ahead, reserve one cup of the broth. Make the risotto as listed prior to the last addition of broth. Spread the risotto on a parchment-lined baking sheet into one layer and secure tightly with plastic wrap. When ready to prepare, bring the reserved broth to a simmer and add the partially cooked risotto. Cook until the liquid is nearly absorbed, stirring constantly. Continue with the remainder of step 3.

Makes 8 servings.
Per Serving: 238 Calories; 8g Fat (31.8% calories from fat); 7g Protein; 31g Carbohydrate; 1g Dietary Fiber; 14mg Cholesterol; 554mg Sodium.

Take this coleslaw to a fish fry for an extra 'bite.'

Tex-Mex Coleslaw

1	onion – peeled and quartered
1	jalapeño pepper – de-stemmed and halved
2	large garlic cloves – peeled
1/2	cup cilantro – leaves and stems
1 1/3	cups safflower oil
1/2	cup red wine vinegar
2	teaspoons sugar
1	teaspoon salt
1	head cabbage – shredded

"Food for thought is no substitute for the real thing."

— Walt Kelly

1. Using a large food processor, drop the onion quarters through the feed tube and pulse to finely chop. Add jalapeño and garlic through the tube and process until minced. Add cilantro and pulse a few times to combine.
2. Add oil, vinegar, sugar and salt and pulse for 5–8 seconds to thoroughly combine mixture.
3. Place cabbage in a large bowl. Pour the processed mixture over the cabbage and toss to combine. Allow flavors to marry for 15 minutes, then serve. Alternately, cover and refrigerate until ready to serve.

Makes 10 servings.
Per Serving: 274 Calories; 29g Fat (93.4% calories from fat); 1g Protein; 4g Carbohydrate; 1g Dietary Fiber; 0mg Cholesterol; 218mg Sodium.

This dish is a big hit at family gatherings.

Proscuitto Wrapped Asparagus with Lemon Butter-Dill Sauce

"My children have taught me how important it is to remember the past and tell its stories, especially at dinner."

— **Eat My Words**
by Janet Theophano

1 1/2	pounds asparagus – rinsed and trimmed
4	slices prosciutto
1	Tablespoon vegetable oil
2	teaspoons garlic oil
1/4	cup chicken broth
1/4	cup unsalted butter
1	Tablespoon lemon juice
3	Tablespoons fresh dill
1	teaspoon lemon zest

1. Preheat oven to 400F.
2. Divide asparagus into 8 even bundles. Cut each proscuitto slice in half lengthwise. Wrap each bundle with the proscuitto and place in a 13 inch x 9 inch glass baking dish. Alternate the tips and ends to promote even cooking.
3. Mix together the garlic and vegetable oils in a small dish. Using a pastry brush, lightly paint the tips and exposed ends of the asparagus with the oil.
4. Pour the chicken broth into the bottom of the baking dish, and place in the oven. Roast for 15 minutes until the stalks are tender.
5. While the asparagus is roasting, melt the butter slowly in a small saucepan. Whisk in the lemon juice and remove from heat. Add the dill and zest. Mix until well combined. When the asparagus emerges from the oven, pour the butter evenly over the prepared asparagus. Serve with a slotted fork.

Makes 8 servings.
Per Serving: 299 Calories; 17g Fat (52.0% calories from fat); 33g Protein; 3g Carbohydrate; 1g Dietary Fiber; 95mg Cholesterol; 3082mg Sodium.

A Caribbean twist on a traditional dish

Orange Wild-Rice Pilaf

- 3 navel oranges
- 1 Tablespoon butter
- 1/4 cup almonds – coarsely chopped
- 1/2 teaspoon ground coriander
- 1/2 teaspoon ground cumin
- 1/2 teaspoon salt
- 1/2 teaspoon black pepper
- 1/8 teaspoon cinnamon
- 1 1/2 cups brown and wild rice blend
- 2 green onions – thinly sliced, (white and green)
- 1/3 cup dried currants – or raisins

1. Working over a glass measuring cup to catch the juice, peel and section 2 of the oranges. Set sections aside in a small dish. From remaining orange, grate enough peel to measure 1/2 teaspoon and add to orange sections. Squeeze juice from the remaining orange into the glass cup. Add enough water to measure 1 3/4 cups liquid. Set juice mixture aside.
2. Melt butter in a saucepan over medium heat. Add almonds and sauté for 2 minutes until golden, stirring constantly. With a slotted spoon, remove almonds to the small dish with the orange sections.
3. In the same saucepan, combine reserved juice mixture, coriander, cumin, salt, pepper, and cinnamon; bring to a boil. Stir in rice blend. Cover and reduce heat to low. Simmer for 40 minutes, or until liquid is absorbed. Remove from heat.
4. Stir in reserved orange sections and orange peels, toasted almonds, scallions and currants. Cover; let stand for 5 minutes before serving.

In 1940, the average American consumed in a year: 154 pounds of fruit and 265 pounds of vegetables.

In 2000, the average American consumed in a year: 279 pounds of fruit (126 of it fresh) and 428 pounds of vegetables (201 of it fresh).

Makes 6 servings.
Per Serving: 280 Calories; 6g Fat (20.0% calories from fat); 7g Protein; 50g Carbohydrate; 6g Dietary Fiber; 5mg Cholesterol; 468mg Sodium.

A touch of cool, best served with a spicy dish.

Cucumber Relish

1	large cucumber – peeled and sliced
1	onion – thinly sliced
1 1/2	teaspoons sugar
1	Tablespoon cider vinegar
1/2	cup plain lowfat yogurt
1/2	teaspoon salt and pepper
2	Tablespoons fresh mint leaves – chopped

1. Mix cucumber, onion, sugar and vinegar together in a medium bowl. Cover and chill.
2. Just before serving, stir cold yogurt into cucumber mixture. Add salt and pepper and garnish with coarsely chopped fresh mint.

The Kitchen Is The Temple Of Life
So much there is that's lovely in a kitchen:
The silver water flowing to my hand,
The golden flame that answers to my fingers,
Row upon row of shining things that stand,
And wait my using in some mystery,
Ancient as Eden, new this very hour.
Here fragrance rises from a darkened cavern,
Strange mingling of flavor and of flour
From waving wheatfield and fruit laden trees.
Here ivory of eggs, and gleaming yolk
Pass through strange alchemy beneath my hands
Who make of them a strengthening for folk.
To the most dear. Beauty there is, and miracle,
Windows where roses nod, a bird's swift wing.
This is my kingdom, yea, my very temple,
Here may I serve and pray. Here may I sing.

— Catherine Cate Coblentz,
American Scientist and Children's Book Author (1897-1951)

Makes 4 servings.
Per Serving: 48 Calories; 1g Fat (11.0% calories from fat); 3g Protein; 9g Carbohydrate; 1g Dietary Fiber; 2mg Cholesterol; 202mg Sodium.

*Caliente Crusted Chicken and a small serving of sliced mango and papaya make this meal colorful **and** delicious.*

What Now?
More heat? Increase the chili powder and chili paste. Then add a few extra drops of vegetable oil in the processor to keep the cakes from cracking when you remove them from the oven.

Black Bean Cakes

- 30 ounces canned black beans – drained and rinsed
- 2 Tablespoons vegetable oil
- 1 Tablespoon chili paste
- 2 Tablespoons chili powder – ancho or chipotle
- 1 Tablespoon ground cumin
- 1/4 cup cilantro – chopped
- 1/2 teaspoon salt – or to taste

1. Preheat oven to 350F.
2. Place the beans and vegetable oil in a food processor, and puree. Add the chili paste, chili powder, cumin, cilantro, and salt. Puree for one minute to combine.
3. Line two baking sheets with parchment paper. Place a 2 Tablespoon size ball of the mixture onto the sheet. Press evenly with a large, flat spatula to make cakes 1/4 inch tall and about 3 to 4 inches across. Repeat using all of the mixture.
4. Bake for 8–10 minutes or until the cakes are warm and will glide easily onto a spatula. Move gently to the plate.

Makes 8 servings.
Per Serving: 133 Calories; 5g Fat (32.7% calories from fat); 6g Protein; 16g Carbohydrate; 7g Dietary Fiber; 0mg Cholesterol; 494mg Sodium.

Greeted by the smell of fresh made bread,
all are assured they are welcomed home.

Turning the dough for the rolls gives it a fresh-baked look across the top.

Simple Whole Wheat Bread

1	package active dry yeast – fast acting
1/2	teaspoon salt
2	Tablespoons sugar
1	Tablespoon wheat gluten – (optional)
1 1/2	cups whole-grain wheat flour
1	cup water – warm (110F)
2 1/2	cups all-purpose flour
1/4	cup water – hot (150F)
3	Tablespoons honey
3	Tablespoons unsalted butter
1	Tablespoon oil – to coat bowl

1. Preheat oven to 350F.
2. In a large stand-up mixer, combine yeast, salt, sugar, gluten and 1/2 cup wheat flour together until ingredients are well incorporated. Add warm water and beat until smooth. Add remaining cup of wheat flour and approximately 2 cups of all-purpose flour to create a soft, workable dough. Cover with a towel; set in warm place for approximately 35 minutes.
3. Combine hot water, butter, and honey. Add to risen dough, and mix in approximately 1/2 cup of all-purpose flour. Turn dough out onto floured surface, and knead until smooth and elastic, about 2–3 minutes. Add flour by Tablespoonfuls if the dough begins to get sticky.
4. Place dough in vegetable oil greased bowl, turning to coat the top. Cover loosely with plastic wrap and a towel. Let rise in a warm place for about 30 minutes, or until doubled in bulk.
5. Turn dough out on board and knead lightly. Using pastry scraper or dull knife, cut dough into 2 equal pieces for two loaves. If preparing rolls, cut into 16 equal pieces and shape into rolls.

6a. (2 Loaves) Put dough into greased loaf pans and score the top. Place in 350F oven for 35 minutes. Remove to racks for cooling.

6b. (16 rolls) Place rolls on cookie sheets and put in 350F oven for 20 minutes. Remove to racks for cooling.

Makes 16 servings.
Per Serving: 159 Calories; 3g Fat (19.4% calories from fat); 4g Protein; 28g Carbohydrate; 2g Dietary Fiber; 6mg Cholesterol; 70mg Sodium.

Very simply put together for the nights of little preparation time.

Sweet Almond Spinach

- 10 ounces spinach leaves – stems removed
- 3 Tablespoons currants
- 1 Tablespoon water – hot (150F)
- 2 Tablespoons extra virgin olive oil
- 1/2 medium onion – cut in 1/2 inch dice
- 3 Tablespoons slivered almonds – toasted
- 1/4 cup cream sherry
- Salt and pepper – to taste

1. Wash the spinach and drain well.
2. Place currants in a small dish. Pour the hot water over them and cover with plastic wrap to soften.
3. Heat the olive oil in a large non-stick frying pan for 20 seconds. Add the onion, and sauté for five minutes or until onions are lightly golden and soft.
4. Add the almonds, currants and sherry to the onions. Stir to combine.
5. Add the drained spinach, and lightly toss the mixture in the skillet. Place a lid on the pan, and cook over low heat for two minutes or until the leaves are just wilted.
6. Sprinkle mixture with salt and pepper, and stir gently to combine. Serve hot or at room temperature.

"In France in the 17th century, they invented the process of taking almonds and rocking them in a bowl, coating them with corn syrup and sugar. That formed a hard candy shell for what is now called Jordan almonds."

— Lance Jensen, President of Modernista! advertising agency

Makes 4 servings.
Per Serving: 135 Calories; 11g Fat (65.5% calories from fat); 3g Protein; 9g Carbohydrate; 3g Dietary Fiber; 0mg Cholesterol; 42mg Sodium.

I found Swiss Chard during a grocery store adventure. I have enjoyed it ever since.

Swiss Chard Sandwich

About 1 bunch of Swiss Chard will yield 10 ounces of leaves, equal to about 7–8 cups of loosely packed leaves.

- 10 ounces Swiss chard
- 1/2 cup walnuts – toasted
- 1 egg – beaten
- 2 cups cooked brown rice
- 2 Tablespoons olive oil
- 1 cup onion – cut in 1/2 inch dice
- 2 Tablespoons fresh ginger – finely chopped
- 4 garlic cloves – minced
- 2 Tablespoons Romano cheese – grated
- 2 Tablespoons lemon juice
- 3 ounces raisins – (2 single serving boxes)
- 1/2 teaspoon salt – (optional)

1. Preheat oven to 350F.
2. Wash greens and shake dry. Cut a V pattern in the chard to remove stems from the leaves. Roughly chop leaves and set aside.
3. Toast walnuts in a dry sauté pan, and grind in food processor until the consistency of dry bread crumbs. Lightly beat the egg, and mix with prepared rice. Add walnuts and mix thoroughly.
4. Heat olive oil; sauté onions until golden. Add ginger and garlic. Toss in the chopped leaves and sauté until wilted. Remove from heat.
5. Toss leaves with lemon juice and raisins. Add salt if desired.
6. Place half of rice mixture in the bottom of an 8 or 9-inch glass pie pan. Layer the chard mixture on top, spreading evenly over the rice. Sprinkle the Romano cheese over the chard mixture. Top with the remaining rice to make the chard-rice sandwich.
7. Bake for 15 minutes, until the top layer seems firm, and you can see the center mixture bubbling.
8. Cut into pie slices to serve.

Makes 8 servings.
Per Serving: 198 Calories; 9g Fat (40.9% calories from fat); 6g Protein; 25g Carbohydrate; 3g Dietary Fiber; 28mg Cholesterol; 108mg Sodium.

The travels of a family cookbook may be irregular, but it was keeping it in motion that mattered in general within a family circle, keeping a woman, a family, and its memories alive.

— **Eat My Words**
by Janet Theophano

Every life should have a recipe that stretches back for generations.

Grandmother Berry's Baked Beans

- 1/2 pound thick-sliced bacon – cut into 1 inch pieces
- 2 medium onions – cut into 1/2 inch dice
- 30 ounces pork and beans – canned
- 3 Tablespoons mustard
- 1 cup chili sauce
- 1 cup brown sugar

1. Preheat oven to 350F.
2. Lightly fry bacon pieces in a large oven safe skillet. Add onions and sauté until golden brown. Add remaining ingredients and stir to combine.
3. Place skillet into the oven and bake for 25 to 30 minutes.

Makes 8 servings.
Per Serving: 365 Calories; 16g Fat (38.1% calories from fat); 15g Protein; 43g Carbohydrate; 7g Dietary Fiber; 32mg Cholesterol; 979mg Sodium.

Whether for New Year's Eve luck or a mid-summer picnic, this dish needs a large serving spoon.

Hoppin' John Black-Eyed Peas

Substitute Canadian bacon to lower the fat content.

Black-eyed peas prepared with ham or bacon are eaten to encourage New Year's luck. The peas represent coins you will receive, while "going whole hog" denotes overall prosperity.

- 1 cup black-eyed peas – frozen or fresh
- 4 slices thick-sliced bacon – cut in 1/2 inch pieces
- 1 cup onion – cut in 1/2 inch dice
- 1/2 cup bell pepper – cut in 1/2 inch dice
- 2 serrano peppers – cut in 1/8 inch slices
- 1 garlic clove – minced
- 2 cups chicken broth
- 1 teaspoon salt
- 1 teaspoon black pepper
- 1/4 teaspoon cayenne pepper
- 1 bay leaf
- 3 cups cooked rice

1. If using fresh black eyes, add to boiling water, and set aside about an hour. If frozen, add boiling water and set aside just while browning vegetables. Drain and rinse.
2. Lightly fry bacon in a 2 quart saucepan until browned. Add onion, bell pepper, serrano and garlic. Sauté until onion is tender.
3. Add peas, chicken broth, spices and bay leaf. Cover and simmer 40 to 50 minutes, or until peas are tender.
4. Remove bay leaf and stir in rice. Simmer 10 more minutes until liquid has been absorbed.

Makes 6 servings.
Per Serving: 291 Calories; 5g Fat (16.5% calories from fat); 14g Protein; 47g Carbohydrate; 4g Dietary Fiber; 7mg Cholesterol; 752mg Sodium.

Add bright colors to your dinner plate with this red and green staircase

Tomate et Courgette Escalier

- 2 Tablespoons vegetable oil
- 1 pound zucchini – sliced 1/4 inch thick
- 1 cup yellow onion – cut in 1/2 inch dice
- 1 1/2 pounds tomatoes – sliced 1/4 inch thick
- 1 Tablespoon olive oil
- 1 teaspoon Herbs de Provence

1. Sauté zucchini slices in vegetable oil until they begin to soften. Remove from pan to cool, leaving as much oil as possible.
2. Using remaining oil, sauté onions until golden. Spread onions in an even layer into an 8 inch square baking dish.
3. Layer alternating zucchini and tomato slices in long rows in the baking dish. Stir together the olive oil and Herbs de Provence. Drizzle mixture over the 'staircase' and set aside until just before serving.
4. Preheat oven to 400F. Place dish in the oven for about 5–8 minutes until tomatoes are hot to the touch. Serve immediately.

Try to get tomatoes not much larger in circumference than the zucchini. In the event you can only get large ones, cut them into half-moons, and show the rounded side up.

A recipe similar to this was taught at Cordon Bleu while I was living in Paris. It is classically French in its flavor and simplicity.

Makes 6 servings.
Per Serving: 102 Calories; 7g Fat (59.4% calories from fat); 2g Protein; 9g Carbohydrate; 2g Dietary Fiber; 0mg Cholesterol; 12mg Sodium.

The two types and colors of squash look beautiful together.

"Just enough food and drink should be taken to restore our strength, and not to overburden it."

— Cicero

Calabacitas

1	pound zucchini – sliced 1/4 inch thick
1	pound yellow squash – sliced 1/4 inch thick
1/4	cup green onion – chopped
2	Tablespoons vegetable oil
1/4	cup lowfat 1% milk
2	cups frozen corn kernels
4	ounces green chiles – canned
1/2	cup queso fresco – shredded

1. In a large skillet, heat oil. Combine squash and onions to sauté for about 3 minutes. Cover and simmer for 5 minutes.
2. Add milk and corn. Cover and simmer until corn is tender and warmed through.
3. Add green chiles. Cover and let simmer for about a minute, then remove from heat.
4. Stir in grated cheese and cover. Allow to sit a few minutes and serve when the cheese has melted.

Makes 6 servings.
Per Serving: 137 Calories; 6g Fat (36.5% calories from fat); 5g Protein; 19g Carbohydrate; 4g Dietary Fiber; 3mg Cholesterol; 24mg Sodium.

Create an autumn marriage of this dense bread and a hearty stew.

Whole Wheat Oatmeal Bread

2 cups boiling water
1 cup rolled oats
1/2 cup honey
2 teaspoons salt
1 Tablespoon butter
1 package dry yeast
1/2 cup warm water – 105F–115 F
2 cups whole wheat flour
2 cups all-purpose flour
1 Tablespoon vegetable oil – (for greasing bowl)
1/2 cup all-purpose flour
2 Tablespoons rolled oats

1. Combine boiling water and oats in a large mixing bowl. Let stand one hour.
2. Stir honey into the oat mixture. In a small bowl, dissolve yeast in warm water and let stand for 5 minutes. Add salt, butter and dissolved yeast to the oat mixture. Stir well.
3. Using an electric mixer, combine the wheat flour with the oat mixture. After a few minutes, start adding the all-purpose flour 1/2 cup at a time until the dough no longer sticks to the side of the bowl.
4. Place dough in a greased bowl. Turn dough over to coat all sides. Cover loosely with a towel, and let rise in a warm place, for about an hour.
5. Punch dough down. Turn dough onto a lightly floured surface, and knead until smooth and elastic. Add up to 1/2 cup flour.
6. Divide dough in half, shaping each half into a loaf. Place in a two well-greased 9 inch x 5 inch loaf pans. Score the bread and sprinkle 1 Tablespoon of oats over each loaf. Cover, and let rise until doubled, about 40 minutes. Preheat oven to 350F about halfway through rising time.
7. Bake loaves at 350F for 50 minutes or until toasty golden.

Toasted slices with fruit preserves make a delicious breakfast.

Baking times may vary for this bread. You may use the 'thump' test. If you can lightly hear the thump, it is ready.

Makes 16 servings.
Per Serving: 191 Calories; 2g Fat (11.1% calories from fat); 5g Protein; 39g Carbohydrate; 3g Dietary Fiber; 2mg Cholesterol; 277mg Sodium.

Saffron Swirl of Couscous

1/2 cup chicken broth
1 teaspoon saffron threads
1/4 teaspoon salt
1/2 cup couscous
1 Tablespoon unsalted butter

1. In a medium saucepan, bring the chicken broth to a boil. Add the saffron. Remove from heat and allow to infuse for 15 minutes.
2. Add salt and return the liquid to a boil. Add the couscous, stirring quickly, and remove from heat. Add butter and continue to stir until all the liquid is absorbed. Fluff with fork and serve.

War having ceased, the camp bore the appearance of a monster banqueting hall. "We have done fighting," said everyone, "so let us terminate the campaign by feasting, lay down our victorious but murderous weapons, and pick up those more useful and restorative arms — the knife and fork ..."

"... I require a base sufficiently strong to resist the joint attacks of the heads of thereof the most powerful armies in the world, and only be destroyed after having conquered the conqueror's place d'armes, the stomach, so called in military parlance." And so was created the Soyer's Culinary Emblem of Peace.

— ***The Emblem of Peace*** (1855) by Alexis Soyer,
First Chapbook for Foodies

Makes 4 servings.
Per Serving: 112 Calories; 3g Fat (26.0% calories from fat); 3g Protein; 17g Carbohydrate; 1g Dietary Fiber; 8mg Cholesterol; 231mg Sodium.

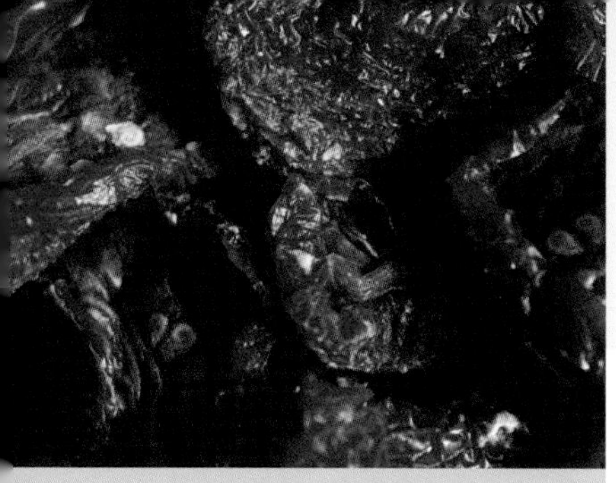

Using two types of sun-dried tomatoes keeps the calorie count down.

Arugula, Sun-Dried Tomato and Rosemary Melange

- 8 ounces sun-dried tomatoes, oil-packed – julienned
- 5 ounces sun-dried tomatoes – julienned
- 3 Tablespoons fresh rosemary – chopped
- 4 cups arugula leaves – about 6 ounces
- 3 Tablespoons pine nuts – toasted
- 1/2 teaspoon salt
- 1/2 teaspoon freshly ground black pepper

1. Strain the oil from the tomato jar into a measuring cup. It should be about 1/4 cup of oil and spices. Add vegetable oil, only if needed. Heat in a medium saucepan over low heat.
2. Add the plain dried tomatoes to the saucepan and heat slowly to soften. Combine rosemary and tomatoes from the jar to the mixture and continue stirring over a low flame until all tomatoes are warm.
3. Add the arugula and toss until just wilted.
4. Add toasted pine nuts, and stir until well combined. Season with salt and pepper. Serve immediately.

Makes 8 servings.
Per Serving: 128 Calories; 6g Fat (38.4% calories from fat); 5g Protein; 18g Carbohydrate; 4g Dietary Fiber; 0mg Cholesterol; 583mg Sodium.

Think of the beautiful swirl of a dancer's skirt when you see the tomatoes gracefully atop the polenta

Smoked Gouda Polenta with Dancing Skirt Tomatoes

2 Tablespoons unsalted butter
1 quart milk
2 cups cream
2 teaspoons sugar
1 teaspoon salt
2 cups cornmeal
1 pound smoked Gouda cheese – shredded
1 quart boiling water
2 pints cherry tomatoes – stems intact
2 Tablespoons extra virgin olive oil
4 cloves garlic – minced

Many types of cheeses can make this dish delicious, such as Italian Caciocavallo and French Comte.

1. Using non-stick spray, prepare a large rimmed cookie sheet for the polenta.
2. Melt butter in a large saucepan. Add milk, cream, sugar and salt. Bring to a gentle simmer and stir in the cornmeal, incorporating quickly with a whisk.
3. After the cornmeal has started to thicken, add the cheese a handful at a time, until it is all melted. Pour onto the cookie sheet and spread evenly to cool.
4. Bring 1 quart water to boil in a deep saucepan. Using the point of a small paring knife, make an X on the bottom of each cherry tomato. Plunge into the boiling water for 3 to 5 seconds, and remove. Gently peel the skin toward the stems and lift. They will look like the twirling skirt of a dancer.
5. In a large sauté pan, heat the oil until it sizzles. Add the garlic and place the tomatoes in the oil. Swirl the hot oil gently to flavor the tomatoes. Remove from heat.
6. Cut 2 inch x 2 inch squares of slightly cooled polenta from the pan. Lift onto plate. Place a few tomatoes over the polenta, and serve.

Makes 16 servings.
Per Serving: 313 Calories; 21g Fat (60.2% calories from fat); 12g Protein; 20g Carbohydrate; 2g Dietary Fiber; 69mg Cholesterol; 423mg Sodium.

Spicy pepperoncini adds a boost to broccoli.

Broccoli-Pepperoncini Sauté

All Saints Day (November 1) finds the French visiting cemeteries of their loved ones, including Le Cimetière des Chiens, in north-western Paris. There you will find beloved pets, statues honoring famous rescue dogs, as well as the grave of Rin-Tin-Tin.

6	cups broccoli florets – including up to 1 inch of tender stem
3	Tablespoons pepperoncini peppers – sliced 1/4 inch thick
1	clove garlic – (from pepperoncini jar), sliced thin
1/2	cup chicken broth
2	Tablespoons vegetable oil

1. Combine peppers, garlic and broth in a small dish.
2. In a large stir-fry pan, heat oil. Quickly toss broccoli in hot oil for about 3 minutes or just until the green starts to shine.
3. Add pepper mixture to the broccoli and stir to combine. Cover for 3–5 minutes until broccoli is steamed to crisp perfection.

Makes 6 servings.
Per Serving: 67 Calories; 5g Fat (60.8% calories from fat); 3g Protein; 4g Carbohydrate; 2g Dietary Fiber; 0mg Cholesterol; 84mg Sodium.

As an alternative to traditional southern cornbread stuffing, it's a fun change.

Wild Rice and Fennel Stuffing

- 1 1/2 cups wild rice
- 1 Tablespoon fennel seed
- 3 cups chicken broth
- 1 1/2 cups water
- 1/2 pound Italian sausage
- 2 Tablespoons unsalted butter
- 2 cups chopped onion
- 2 cups fennel – (about 3 bulbs) cut in 1/2 inch dice
- Salt and pepper – to taste

1. In a medium-sized saucepan, combine the wild rice, fennel seed, broth and water and bring the liquid to a boil. Reduce the heat, partially cover the pan and simmer the rice for 45 to 55 minutes or until it is tender. Set the rice aside.
2. In a heavy skillet, brown and crumble the sausage. Drain fat and allow to rest on paper towels to absorb remaining fat.
3. Melt butter in the skillet and sauté the onion over medium heat until it is soft, about 5 minutes. Add the fennel, and stir to combine. Cover the pan and allow to simmer together for about 7 or 8 minutes until the fennel is tender-crisp.
4. Combine the fennel mixture, sausage and rice into a large bowl. Add salt and pepper, and toss to combine the ingredients. Serve warm.

Wild rice is a long grain marsh grass traditionally harvested by being tapped with an oar while in a canoe. Imagine that!

If fennel is difficult to find, use celery and add 1 additional Tablespoon of dried fennel seeds.

Makes 12 servings.
Per Serving: 180 Calories; 9g Fat (42.2% calories from fat); 7g Protein; 19g Carbohydrate; 2g Dietary Fiber; 20mg Cholesterol; 340mg Sodium.

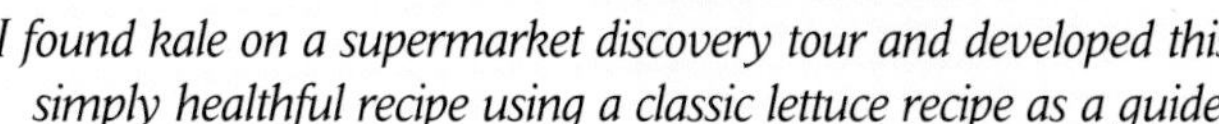

I found kale on a supermarket discovery tour and developed this simply healthful recipe using a classic lettuce recipe as a guide.

Wilted Asian Kale

- 4 cups kale – washed and trimmed
- 2 Tablespoons salad vinegar
- 1 Tablespoon sesame oil
- 1 teaspoon sugar
- 1/2 teaspoon Chinese five spice
- 1/4 cup pine nuts – toasted

1. Tear greens into bite size pieces in a large bowl.
2. Put vinegar, sesame oil, sugar and five spice into a very small saucepan. Heat until it begins to bubble and sugar is completely dissolved.
3. Pour over kale and toss until the liquid covers all the leaves.
4. Sprinkle in the pine nuts and serve.

If you prefer this as traditional warm wilted lettuce, microwave the greens (while still damp) on high for no more than 15 seconds. Then continue with step two.

Makes 6 servings.
Per Serving: 59 Calories; 4g Fat (57.5% calories from fat); 2g Protein; 5g Carbohydrate; 1g Dietary Fiber; 0mg Cholesterol; 15mg Sodium.

Bow-tie pasta also works well with this dish.

Broccoli and Garlic Penne

The variety of leftover steamed green vegetables from your refrigerator can be used in place of the broccoli

16 ounces penne pasta
2 Tablespoons unsalted butter
4 cups broccoli flowerets
1/4 cup extra virgin olive oil
10 large cloves garlic – thinly sliced, crosswise
1/2 teaspoon freshly ground black pepper – to taste
2 Tablespoons unsalted butter
1/2 cup Parmesan cheese – freshly grated

1. Bring a large pot of water to a boil. Add the penne, and cook at a rolling boil until the pasta is just tender. Drain and toss with 2 Tablespoons butter.
2. Plunge broccoli into the boiling salted pasta water. Simmer for 3 minutes. Drain, and reserve.
3. In a large skillet, and heat oil over medium heat for about a minute. Add the garlic slices, stirring until the garlic begins to brown around the edges. Guard against burning the garlic.
4. Add the broccoli to the skillet. Toss generously and add pepper. Cook for an additional 2 minutes.
5. Add the penne to the broccoli. Stir the mixture together and add the additional 2 Tablespoons of butter. Continue to stir over the heat until the entire mixture is hot.
6. Pour into a serving bowl and add Parmesan cheese. Serve warm.

What if we were more afraid of not trying and having to live with the thought of "What if?" We decided to give it our all, and take pride in simply doing our best. "Si on n'essaie pas, on ne le saura jamais!" we said — "If we don't try, we'll never know!"

— From a web travelogue

Makes 8 servings.
Per Serving: 360 Calories; 15g Fat (37.4% calories from fat); 11g Protein; 46g Carbohydrate; 3g Dietary Fiber; 19mg Cholesterol; 108mg Sodium.

Slice and serve with a crispy Italian salad

Pepperoni-Cheese Bread

- 1/3 cup water — warm (110F)
- 1 teaspoon sugar
- 1 package active dry yeast
- 1 cup milk
- 1 teaspoon salt
- 1 cup cheddar cheese — grated
- 2 ounces pepperoni slices — finely chopped
- 3 1/2 cups all-purpose flour

1. In a small bowl, stir together the water, sugar, and yeast. Let stand 5 minutes, stirring occasionally, until mixture is foamy.
2. In a large bowl, stir together milk and salt. Pour in yeast mixture. Add cheese and pepperoni.
3. Add 2 1/2 cups flour and blend until smooth. Stir in as much of the remaining flour as necessary to form a soft dough.
4. Turn dough out onto lightly floured (2 Tablespoons) board. Knead 7 to 10 minutes, adding remaining flour as necessary until the dough is no longer sticky.
5. Place in lightly greased bowl. Turn dough once to coat. Cover with plastic wrap. Allow to rise in a warm place for about an hour, or until double in bulk.
6. Preheat oven to 400F. Prepare two loaf pans with non-stick spray.
7. Punch down dough and turn out onto lightly floured board. Divide dough in half. Roll each half into a loaf 2 inches shorter than the pan. Bake for 1 hour, or until bread is golden brown. Remove from loaf pans and cool on a wire rack.

A Mid-Life Crisis. It's at that midpoint in our personal continuum when our lives hang in delicate balance and we look behind to see how far we've come and realize that our past is no longer a solitary trail through secret woods but a vista as big and expansive as the ocean itself, stretching to the horizons with our experiences, nothing more than tiny, dot-like sailboats swallowed up by the enormous sea.

— "Chris In The Morning" of **Northern Exposure**

Makes 12 servings.
Per Serving: 210 Calories; 6g Fat (27.3% calories from fat); 8g Protein; 30g Carbohydrate; 1g Dietary Fiber; 16mg Cholesterol; 344mg Sodium.

Courge à la Mangue

- 6 pounds spaghetti squash – cut in half lengthwise
- 1 Tablespoon olive oil
- 6 ounces bacon – 1/2 inch dice
- 1 cup celery – 1/2 inch dice
- 1/2 cup onion – 1/2 inch dice
- 1/2 cup shallot – 1/2 inch dice
- 1/2 cup carrot – 1/2 inch dice
- 2 cloves garlic – minced
- 1 medium potato – cut in 1 inch pieces
- 2 cups chicken broth
- 1 large mango – seeded and sliced
- 4 cups chicken broth
- 1/2 cup heavy cream

1. Preheat oven to 350F. Place spaghetti squash on a baking sheet and roast until fork tender, about 45 minutes. Remove from oven and allow to cool.
2. Put diced bacon in a heavy bottommed soup pot. As it begins to curl, pour off the bacon drippings and discard. Continue cooking the bacon, and add the onion, carrot, celery, and garlic. Sauté the vegetables until the onion is lightly golden in color.
3. Add the diced potato and the chicken broth to the mixture. Let simmer for about 10 minutes.
4. Break open the cooled squash. Dice and add to the soup pot. Stir in the mangoes with their liquid, and the additional 4 cups of broth. Simmer another 5 minutes or until the squash is warmed throughout.
5. Carefully spoon the mixture into a heavy blender in batches, and puree smooth. [Use caution with the hot liquids, as they can make the blender top pop off without warning.]
6. Return pureed mixture to the soup pot and heat to a gentle boil. (Add more broth at this point for a thinner soup) Just prior to serving, remove from heat, and stir in 1/2 cup cream. Ladle into bowls.

For a leaner version of this recipe, use Canadian Bacon in place of regular bacon.

If mangoes are out of season, a jar or can of mangoes can be used.

Makes 6 servings.
Per Serving: 493 Calories; 28g Fat (48.5% calories from fat); 18g Protein; 48g Carbohydrate; 2g Dietary Fiber; 51mg Cholesterol; 1326mg Sodium.

Rich red strips with long cream colored ribbons

Fettuccini Rouge

1	pound fettuccine – uncooked
2	Tablespoons oil – from sun-dried tomato jar
2	cloves garlic – minced
1	teaspoon dried oregano
8	ounces sun-dried tomatoes, oil-packed – cut in quarters, (reserve oil)
15	ounces jarred roasted red peppers – drained and cut into strips
1	teaspoon oil – from sun-dried tomato jar
1/4	cup grated Parmesan cheese

1. In a large pasta pot, bring 3 quarts of water to a rapid boil. Prepare pasta according to package directions.
2. Heat the oil in a 2 quart saucepan. Add additional vegetable oil, only if needed. Sauté the garlic and add oregano. Stir sun-dried tomatoes into mixture, and then gently add roasted peppers. Cover and keep warm until the pasta is prepared.
3. Add 1 teaspoon of oil to a large bowl. Remove pasta to the bowl and coat with the oil. Use vegetable oil if the jar did not have enough oil.
4. Pour the warm sauce over the fettuccini. Mix thoroughly.
5. Sprinkle with cheese and serve.

For really good cooks, it is the preparation of meals that arouses excitement and anticipation, the experimentation with new combinations, exoticism of a domestic sort. In Huysman's "A Rebours (Against the Grain)" involving as it does in one passage of inspired silliness, the Decadent hero "playing internal symphonies to himself by providing his palate with sensations analogous to those which music dispenses to the ear."

— **Food for Thought: The Meaning of Eating** by Joyce Carol Oates

Makes 8 servings.
Per Serving: 333 Calories; 10g Fat (25.7% calories from fat); 10g Protein; 53g Carbohydrate; 4g Dietary Fiber; 2mg Cholesterol; 127mg Sodium.

Potée Française
Mother's Golden Chicken Soup
Roasted
Pumpkin-Apricot Soup
Rancher's Caldillo with Tamale Puffs

Simmering Sumptuousness

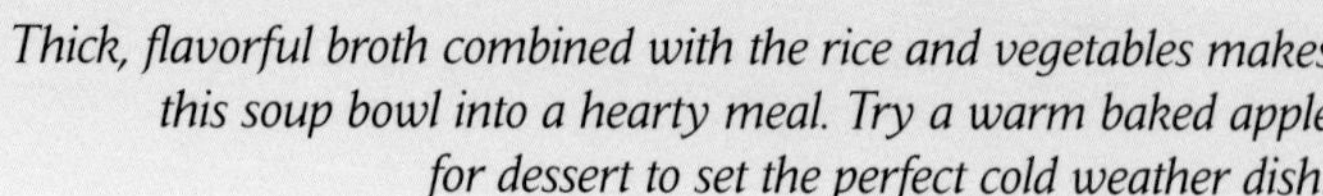

Thick, flavorful broth combined with the rice and vegetables makes this soup bowl into a hearty meal. Try a warm baked apple for dessert to set the perfect cold weather dish.

Twin Cities Wild Rice Soup

4 cups chicken broth
3/4 cup wild rice
5 cups chicken broth – hot
3 strips bacon, thick-sliced – 1/2 inch pieces
1/4 cup ham – 1/4 inch dice
1 cup onion – 1/4 inch dice
1/2 cup carrot – 1/4 inch dice
1/4 cup celery, 1/4 inch dice
1/4 cup flour – (up to 1/2 cup)
1 Tablespoon Worcestershire sauce
1 teaspoon Tabasco® sauce
1 cup heavy cream – (or whole milk)
salt and pepper

1. In a large saucepot, prepare the rice with 4 cups of chicken broth. When the rice is tender (about 45 minutes to an hour), drain remaining broth into a large measuring cup. Remove the prepared rice to a bowl.
2. In a stockpot, heat the remaining rice liquid, plus additional chicken broth to make 5 cups total. Heat to a warm simmer.
3. In a heavy soup pot over medium heat, sauté bacon and ham together until the bacon is cooked, but not crisp.
4. Add the onion, carrot and celery. Stir and cook for about 3 minutes; carrots will still feel firm. Add 2 Tablespoons flour to make a small roux. (Additional flour is only required if the vegetables are not well coated by the roux.) Stir and cook up to 3 additional minutes.
5. Add the cooked rice, Worcestershire, Tabasco,® and 1 cup of the hot chicken stock. Whisk away any lumps of flour. Add the remaining broth and bring to a boil. Allow to simmer 3–5 minutes. If soup seems too thin, remove about a half cup of the hot broth to mix with a tablespoon or two of flour, and add back to the soup pot. Simmer 2–3 minutes more to remove the raw flour taste.
6. Just prior to serving, remove from heat and stir in the cream. Taste and season with salt and pepper, if necessary. Serve in bowls warm from the oven.

Makes 6 servings.
Per Serving: 349 Calories; 21g Fat (53.5% calories from fat); 15g Protein; 26g Carbohydrate; 2g Dietary Fiber; 63mg Cholesterol; 1373mg Sodium.

Wild rice is not really a rice. It is a long grain marsh grass with a nutty flavor and chewy texture.

Roux: A mixture of equal parts of fat and flour, cooked until bubbly and light brown.

If the wild rice is made in advance, you are less than thirty minutes to having dinner ready.

What now?
Pesky lumps of flour? Using a fork or a whisk, make the soup smooth in step 5 before you add the remaining broth. It makes a big difference.

Orzo is a small, rice-shaped pasta

For the nights not everyone makes it to the table at the same time, this dish holds well on the stove. It can also be reheated the next day for a filling lunch.

Main Dish Minestrone

6	Tablespoons unsalted butter
2	cups onion – diced
1 1/2	cups carrots – sliced
1	cup celery – chopped
2	garlic cloves, minced
3	cups beef broth
1	cup water
1 1/2	pounds cabbage, coarsely chopped
15	ounces canned tomatoes
1/3	cup orzo
2	zucchini, cut in 1/2 inch pieces
2	teaspoons salt
2	teaspoons Worcestershire sauce
1/2	teaspoon dried oregano
1/4	teaspoon pepper
30	ounces red kidney beans, canned, drained
10	ounces fresh spinach, cut in strips
1/2	cup Parmesan cheese

1. In a large pot, melt butter. Sauté onion, carrots, celery, and garlic until golden, stirring frequently, about 10–15 minutes.
2. Add broth, water, cabbage, tomatoes, zucchini, orzo, salt, Worcestershire sauce, oregano and pepper. Bring to a boil, then reduce heat, cover and simmer 30 minutes or until vegetables are tender.
3. Stir in kidney beans and spinach. Simmer until the beans are heated through. Sprinkle with Parmesan cheese and serve.

Serve with toasted whole grain bread and a hearty red wine.

Makes 10 servings.
Per Serving: 251 Calories; 9g Fat (31.0% calories from fat); 13g Protein; 32g Carbohydrate; 10g Dietary Fiber; 22mg Cholesterol; 1244mg Sodium.

This meal was served the first time I had the courage to invite a chef to dinner. Stew-pendous!

Golden Lamb Stew

- 1 cup black beans – dried
- 1/2 cup golden raisins
- 1/4 cup bourbon
- 1/4 cup hot water
- 2 pounds lamb shoulder, cut in 1 inch cubes
- 1 cup orange juice
- 4 cloves garlic – minced
- 1/4 cup olive oil
- 1 cup pearl onions – or chopped onions
- 1 Tablespoon flour
- 2 teaspoons coriander
- 2 teaspoons thyme
- 1 teaspoon cumin
- 1/2 cup almonds – slivered
- 1/2 cup red wine
- salt and pepper – ground, to taste
- 3 medium tomatoes – seeded, cubed
- 1/2 cup Kalamata olives – halved and pitted
- 2 Tablespoons lemon juice
- 3 Tablespoons cream sherry

To easily seed a tomato, slice it in half horizontally. Standing over a sink or wastebasket, squeeze the tomato to loosen the seeds and give it one forceful shake to release them.

The sweetness of the raisins caramelizes with the cream sherry to balance the saltiness of the olives.

1. Place raisins in a glass bowl, pour the bourbon over and stir to separate the raisins. Add 1/4 cup hot (not boiling) water and give a quick stir. Cover with plastic wrap for at least 30 minutes while preparing other ingredients.
2. Marinate the lamb with the orange juice and garlic in a non-reactive pan for at least two hours in the refrigerator. Drain well and reserve the marinade.
3. Heat two tablespoons of the olive oil in a Dutch oven. Sear the lamb on all sides in small batches. Remove the meat with a slotted spoon to a bowl. Pour the accumulated broth into the orange juice marinade. Do not wash pan.
4. Using the remaining two tablespoons of oil, sauté the onions in the pan until light golden. Sprinkle the flour and spices over the onions and sauté for about three minutes. Add the almonds and cook one minute more.
5. Pour in the red wine, and quickly de-glaze the pan by scraping the bits from the bottom and sides of the pan. Add the raisins with the sherry and the reserved marinade; stir well and season to taste with salt and pepper.
6. Return the lamb to the pot. Add the tomatoes and the olives, stirring to combine. Simmer for about an hour until the meat is tender.
7. Just before serving, add three tablespoons of cream sherry. Ladle into bowls.

Makes 6 servings.
Per Serving: 595 Calories; 41g Fat (65.4% calories from fat); 24g Protein; 25g Carbohydrate; 3g Dietary Fiber; 86mg Cholesterol; 163mg Sodium.

Jane Brody made living the high carbohydrate way a low-fat option. I still love her stuff, even when it's not popular.

Curried Broccoli Soup

1 Tablespoon unsalted butter
1 cup onion – chopped
2 cloves garlic – chopped
1 large potato – peeled and cut into 1/2 inch cubes
3 Tablespoons curry powder
2 cups chicken broth
1 cup water
1 bunch broccoli – cut into florets; stems cut in 1/2 inch slices
freshly ground black pepper, to taste
1 cup milk

1. In a large saucepan, melt the butter. Add the onions and garlic and sauté until the onions are translucent.
2. Add the curry and diced potatoes. The edge of the potato pieces will be firm in about 2–3 minutes. Add the broth and water to the pan. Bring the soup to a boil.
3. Add the broccoli. When the mixture returns to a boil, reduce the heat, cover and simmer for 20 minutes or until the vegetables are tender.
4. Purée the soup in batches in a blender or food processor. Return the purée to the pan, stir in the milk, and taste for seasoning. Warm the soup over low heat. Do not boil to avoid curdling the milk.

Curry can range from mild to very spicy.

By searing the edges of the potato first, it tightens the starches and natural sugars in the potato, giving a much thicker soup.

Makes 6 servings.
Per Serving: 121 Calories; 5g Fat (31.1% calories from fat); 7g Protein; 16g Carbohydrate; 5g Dietary Fiber; 11mg Cholesterol; 307mg Sodium.

Potato soup is steamy comfort in every spoon.

Baked Potato Bowl

3	pounds potatoes – about 4 large
1	Tablespoon unsalted butter
4	pieces thick-sliced bacon – about 4 ounces
1 1/2	cups yellow onion – diced
3	cups chicken broth
1	clove garlic – minced
1	teaspoon white pepper
1/2	teaspoon salt
1	teaspoon dried basil
1/2	teaspoon Tabasco sauce
1	cup sharp cheddar cheese – grated
2	cups milk
1	cup sour cream
1	cup cheddar cheese, white – grated
1/2	cup green onions, both green and white portions – chopped

1. Preheat oven to 350F. Scrub potatoes well. Prick the skin with a fork to allow steam to escape. Lightly coat with butter and wrap tightly in foil. Bake for approximately 1 hour, or until potato is tender.
2. Peel and dice one potato, about 3/4 cup, and cover with plastic wrap until step 6. Neatly cut 3 remaining potatoes in half lengthwise. Using a spoon or a melon baller, scoop out the center to make the potato bowl.
3. In a 3 quart or medium soup pot, cook bacon until crisp. Remove with a slotted spoon and set aside with the reserved potato. Discard all but 1 tablespoon of the bacon fat from the pot. Add diced onion and sauté until translucent, but not golden. Add chicken broth, garlic, spices and potatoes. Bring to a boil.
4. Prepare the potato bowls. Divide one cup of sharp cheddar cheese over the potato skins. Broil until the cheese has melted into the skins. Place one potato skin in the center of each soup bowl.

You want approximately 4 cups of potatoes, plus the 3/4 cup reserved dice.

Why bother with finding white cheddar? The creamy white soup looks more like liquid potatoes in a crisp sharp cheddar shell. Besides, it's fun to try something new!

Why yellow onions? Their anti-oxidant properties are a benefit for this carbohydrate rich meal.

5. After the soup has come to a boil, remove from heat. Purée in batches in a blender. [Use caution when using hot liquids in the blender; the top can pop off without warning] Return to pot, stir in the milk and sour cream. Bring to a low simmer. Add 1 cup of white cheddar (or Monterey Jack cheese), a little at a time until it is all melted into the soup.
6. Gently stir in bacon, reserved diced potatoes, and green onions. Remove from heat, and taste for salt. Ladle soup into the bowl filling up to the edge of the potato skin. Serve.

"We may live without poetry, music and art;
We may live without conscience, and live without heart;
We may live without friends; we may live without books;
But civilized man cannot live without cooks."

— Owen Meredith

Makes 6 servings.
Per Serving: 569 Calories; 30g Fat (47.4% calories from fat); 24g Protein; 52g Carbohydrate; 5g Dietary Fiber; 75mg Cholesterol; 1029mg Sodium.

A bit of bisque with a kick, and beautiful in the bowl.

Boisterous Black Bean Bisque

1 pound black beans – soaked overnight
1/4 cup olive oil
1 cup celery – diced
1 1/2 cups onion, diced
4 cloves garlic – cut in half
2 quarts vegetable broth
3 serrano peppers – halved & seeded
1 Tablespoon dried oregano
10 sprigs cilantro – reserving 10 pretty leaves
salt and white pepper – to taste
dash Tabasco® sauce – to taste

1. In a large pan, heat the oil over medium heat until lightly smoking. Add the celery, onions, and garlic. Cook until the onions become translucent, about 3 to 5 minutes.
2. Add the broth, black beans, serranos, and oregano. Bring the liquid to a boil.
3. Reduce the heat and simmer for 1 to 1 1/2 hours, stirring periodically. When the beans are tender, add the cilantro stems.
4. Transfer to a blender and purée for 3 minutes until smooth. Return to pan, season with salt, pepper, and Tabasco® sauce. Bring the soup to a simmer over low heat.
5. Ladle into warm bowls and gently place a cilantro leaf on each.

If bisque is made ahead of time and refrigerated, it may be necessary to thin with a few tablespoons of water or broth before reheating.

What now?

Uh-oh. Did you forget to soak the beans? Pick through the beans and rinse thoroughly. Place in a large bowl and pour in boiling water. Quickly cover with plastic wrap and let sit for 20–30 minutes. Drain and discard water. Repeat with a new batch of boiling water. Cover for 15–20 minutes, then drain and proceed as usual.

Makes 10 servings.
Per Serving: 352 Calories; 9g Fat (23.2% calories from fat); 15g Protein; 54g Carbohydrate; 11g Dietary Fiber; 2mg Cholesterol; 1319mg Sodium.

The flavor-filled broth soups in Asian restaurants are quite easy to prepare at home

S-s-s Soup

10	cups water
4	inch square cheesecloth & cotton string
2	eggs, scrambled dry
2	Tablespoons vegetable oil
1 1/2	cups carrot, cut in 1/2 inch slices
1/2	cup red onion – diced
1/2	cup onion – diced
2	inches lemongrass, cut lengthwise
1/2	pound raw shrimp, (21–25 count)
1/4	teaspoon salt
1	serrano pepper – seeded
1/2	teaspoon salt
8	slices pickled sushi ginger – cut in half

1. In a large stockpot, bring 10 cups of water to a boil.
2. In a non-stick saucepan, scramble the two eggs. Scrape into a 4 inch square piece of cheesecloth and tie closed with a cotton string. Float in the boiling water. Wipe saucepan with a paper towel.
3. Heat oil in the saucepan. Sauté onions and carrots until the onions are translucent, about 3 to 5 minutes. Add to boiling water along with the sliced lemongrass. Boil gently for 15 minutes to impart flavors.
4. Peel, de-vein, and wash shrimp. Cut into small 1/2 inch pieces, about 5 per shrimp. Season with 1/4 teaspoon salt. Cover and refrigerate.
5. Seed the serrano pepper. Cut the serrano pepper into at least 8 pencil thin slices. Set aside.
6. Pour boiled soup through a strainer and return to pot. Discard solids. Return broth to a boil. Add shrimp and serranos. Boil for about 30–45 seconds or until the shrimp begin to turn pink. Remove from heat.
7. Layer two small pieces of sushi ginger in the bottom of each bowl. Divide the serrano slices, and cooked shrimp evenly among all bowls. Ladle hot broth over and serve.

Pickled ginger can be found in the Asian section of your grocery store

"When it rains, the ground is hard." In earthquake prone Japan, a new home's foundation must receive one natural rain before the remainder of the house can be built. This phrase is used as a marriage blessing as well. The initial argument that upsets a new wife to tears is known as the first rain. When the couple makes up, the foundation of the marriage is now as solid as their new home.

Makes 10 servings.
Per Serving: 105 Calories; 5g Fat (44.7% calories from fat); 8g Protein; 7g Carbohydrate; 1g Dietary Fiber; 96mg Cholesterol; 278mg Sodium.

Low in fat, high in fiber. I would say you can relax by the fireplace a few extra minutes!

Vegetarian Ragoût

- 1 cup black beans – dried
- 2 teaspoons dried thyme
- 3 chicken bouillon cubes – crushed
- 2 cups water
- 1 cup onion – diced
- 3/4 cup carrot – diced
- 1/2 cup celery – diced
- 28 ounces canned tomatoes, roughly chopped
- 1 jalapeño – flowered
- 1 garlic clove – minced
- 2 Tablespoons tomato paste
- 3/4 teaspoon dried oregano
- 1/2 teaspoon dried coriander
- 1/2 teaspoon black pepper
- 1 bay leaf
- dash cloves
- 4 cups potato – diced
- 2 Tablespoons vegetable oil
- 1 teaspoon tumeric
- 2 dashes cayenne
- 1/4 teaspoon salt
- 2 cups zucchini – diced
- 3/4 cup red bell peppers, diced
- 1 garlic clove – minced
- 8 ounces yogurt – (optional)

1. Pick over dried black beans and remove pebbles. Place beans in microwave safe bowl. Add dried thyme, cover with water, and seal with plastic wrap. Microwave on High for about 10 minutes. Drain and put in large stew pot.
2. Into the pot, add bouillon cubes, water, onion, carrot, celery, tomatoes, garlic, tomato paste, oregano, coriander, pepper, bay leaf, and cloves into the pot. Stir and mix thoroughly. Float the flowered jalapeño in the stew mixture. Bring to a boil. Reduce the heat, cover and simmer for 30 minutes.
3. In a skillet, heat 2 Tablespoons oil. In a small bowl, toss the potatoes with the tumeric, cayenne, and salt until well covered. Sauté potatoes in hot oil until the edges become translucent. Add to stew pot. Stir to incorporate.
4. In same skillet, (without cleaning it), sauté zucchini, bell pepper, and garlic. Add to stew pot. Stir to incorporate.
5. Check potatoes for tenderness. Remove jalapeño and bay leaf. Serve in warm bowls with dollop of sour cream or yogurt on top.

Flowered jalapeño: *Cut the stem of the jalapeño as close as possible. About halfway down the jalapeño, (or higher, depending on desired heat) make 6–8 cuts to the tip to make the jalapeño appear to be a closed tulip.*

Any kind of dried beans can be substituted.
I really like the spunk added by the black beans.

Makes 6 servings.
Per Serving: 322 Calories; 7g Fat (18.8% calories from fat); 13g Protein; 55g Carbohydrate; 10g Dietary Fiber; 5mg Cholesterol; 744mg Sodium.

If there is ever any leftover white wine, this is a perfect place to give the bottle its finale.

The apples and pears add a delightful hint of sweetness. If the cabbage seems "strong" you may want to try the apricots for their extra sweetness next time to balance the flavor.

Each region of France has its own signature type of stew, or potée. This northern France version is quite filling.

Potée Française

1	cup apples, dried – (pears or apricots)
1 1/3	cups water – approximately
2	Tablespoons butter
2	cups carrots – sliced
1/2	cup celery – diced
2	leeks – cut in 1/2 inch lengths
1/2	pound bacon slices – cut in 1 inch pieces
2/3	cup white wine – divided use
14 1/2	ounces canned new potatoes – whole
3/4	pound smoked sausage – cut in 1 inch pieces
1/2	head cabbage – cut in wedges

1. Place fruit in glass bowl and add 1 cup of water (or more) to cover the fruit. Place plastic wrap over the fruit. Let stand for 12 hours, or microwave for 30 seconds, and let stand while preparing other ingredients.
2. Melt butter in sauté pan. Add carrots, celery, and leeks. Sauté and stir for about 10 minutes.
3. Add bacon pieces, and let them begin to curl. Drain and reserve liquid from the fruit. Add fruit, 1/3 cup of the wine, and 2/3 cup of the fruit water. Cover. Heat to boiling; reduce heat. Simmer for 20 minutes.
4. Add potatoes, remaining wine, and 2/3 cup of the remaining fruit water. Stir the sausage into the mixture.
5. Place cabbage on top of stew, in a single layer, as much as it is possible. Raise heat gently. Simmer for about 10 minutes, covered.
6. Check cabbage with a fork to test for tenderness, and remove from heat when fork easily pierces the core of the cabbage wedge. Season with salt and pepper. Serve in large flat bowls.

Makes 8 servings.
Per Serving: 442 Calories; 30g Fat (62.5% calories from fat); 16g Protein; 24g Carbohydrate; 3g Dietary Fiber; 62mg Cholesterol; 922mg Sodium.

Tortilla soup is the hallmark of an outstanding Mexican restaurant. Try this version of mine.

Fiery Fiesta Soup

Leftover chicken from the Sunday roaster is great for this soup.

To flower a jalapeño: *Cut the stem of a jalapeño as close as possible. About halfway down the jalapeño, (or higher, depending on desired heat) make 6–8 cuts to the tip to make the jalapeño appear to be a closed tulip.*

- 5 cups chicken broth
- 14 ounces vegetable broth – canned
- 1 1/2 Tablespoons garlic
- 1 cup onion, 1/2 inch dice
- 1/2 cup bell pepper, 1/2 inch dice
- 1/2 cup celery, 1/2 inch dice
- 15 ounces hominy, canned – drained and rinsed
- 11 ounces tomato purée
- 11 ounces V-8® vegetable juice – spicy
- 3 Tablespoons chili powder
- 1 Tablespoon cumin
- 1 teaspoon dried oregano
- 1 teaspoon cayenne pepper
- 1/2 teaspoon salt
- 1 jalapeño, flowered, see directions
- 1 jalapeño, seeded and chopped
- 1 Tablespoon masa harina
- 2 cups of chicken, skinned, cooked, and diced
- 1 cup Monterey jack cheese – shredded
- 1/2 cup cheddar cheese – shredded
- 1 cup tomato – seeded and diced
- 1/2 cup cilantro – chopped
- 4 corn tortillas, cut in 1/2 inch strips
- 2 Tablespoons oil
- 1 large lime – cut in 8 wedges

1. In a large soup pot, combine the chicken broth and vegetable broth and bring to a boil.
2. Add garlic, onion, bell pepper, celery, hominy, tomato purée, vegetable juice, dried spices, and chopped jalapeño to the soup. Float the flowered jalapeno in the soup pot. Bring to a simmer.
3. Remove about 1/2 cup of hot broth from the soup. Mix with the masa harina to make a thick, flowable mixture. Return masa blend to the soup and stir. Add diced chicken. Lower heat and simmer slowly while preparing the tortillas.

4. In a small frying pan, heat the oil. Gently fry the tortilla strips until light brown. Using tongs, remove the strips to paper towels to drain.
5. Remove the soup from the heat. Discard the floating jalapeño. Stir in the cheeses, fresh tomato, and cilantro.
6. Ladle into soup bowls and squeeze one lime wedge over each bowl. Top with a few tortillas and serve.

What now?

If you use all chicken broth, it's a little overwhelming with the strong flavor. No vegetable broth available? Use 2 cups of plain water and throw in rough chopped pieces of carrot and celery. Remove them after the broth boils in step one.

If the spicy V-8® is not available, add a few dashes (be bold!) of Tabasco.®

Makes 8 servings.
Per Serving: 392 Calories; 20g Fat (45.2% calories from fat); 21g Protein; 34g Carbohydrate; 6g Dietary Fiber; 59mg Cholesterol; 1561mg Sodium.

This rich autumn soup is mm-mm-gourd, and makes an excellent first course for a Thanksgiving meal.

Roasted Pumpkin-Apricot Soup

- 6 pounds pumpkin – quartered and seeded
- 6 strips bacon, thick-sliced – diced
- 1 cup onion – diced
- 1 cup celery – diced
- 1/2 cup carrot – diced
- 2 cloves garlic – minced
- 2 cups chicken broth
- 1 medium potato, peeled and cut in 1/2 inch dice
- 1/4 cup apricot halves, cut in 1/2 inch pieces
- 4 cups chicken broth
- 1/2 cup heavy cream

1. Preheat oven to 350 F. Place pumpkin on a cookie sheet or in a roasting pan and roast until fork tender, about 30 minutes. Remove from oven and allow to cool.
2. Put diced bacon in the heavy bottom soup pot. As it begins to curl, pour off the bacon drippings and discard. Continue cooking the bacon, and add the onion, carrot, celery, and garlic. Sauté the vegetables until onion is lightly golden in color.
3. Add the diced potato and the chicken broth to the mixture, and let simmer for about 10 minutes.
4. Skin the cooled pumpkin. Dice and add to the soup pot. Stir in the apricots, and the additional 4 cups of broth. Simmer another 5 minutes or until the pumpkin is warmed throughout.
5. Carefully spoon the mixture into a heavy blender in batches, and purée smooth. Use caution with the hot liquids that can make the blender top pop off without warning.
6. Return puréed mixture to the soup pot and heat to a gentle boil. (Add more broth at this point if you like a thinner soup) Just prior to serving, remove from heat, and stir in 1/2 cup cream. Ladle into bowls.

The Vitamin A and Potassium in each serving provides more than half of your daily requirements!

Makes 6 servings.
Per Serving: 357 Calories; 15g Fat (36.7% calories from fat); 15g Protein; 45g Carbohydrate; 5g Dietary Fiber; 38mg Cholesterol; 1002mg Sodium.

If pumpkin is out of season, substitute with two butternut squashes plus one acorn squash. Cut in half and roast for the same 30 minutes on a cookie sheet.

For a lower fat version of this recipe, use Canadian bacon in place of regular bacon.

What now?
Have you have 'crisped' the bacon a little too far?? ***START OVER*** because the burned flavor of the bacon will come through the finished dish. I prefer using thick sliced bacon, because I tend to have a better chance of forgiveness if I am distracted in the kitchen.

Add a hearty whole grain bread and tossed salad to make this a complete meal.

Chicken Mushroom Barley Soup

1 1/2	pounds skinless chicken thighs
1/2	pound mushrooms – sliced thin
1	cup carrots, sliced 1/4 inch thick
1/2	cup celery – chopped
1/2	cup barley – uncooked
1	Tablespoon seasoned salt
1	dash pepper
1/2	cup spinach leaves

1. Place the skinned chicken in a large stockpot, and add water to cover. Bring to a boil. Skim the accumulated foam from the top of the pot and discard.
2. Add remaining ingredients (except spinach) to the water and simmer for an hour.
3. Remove chicken and shred coarsely. Skim off the fat and simmer an additional 15 minutes.
4. Cut spinach into strips. Add chicken and fresh spinach. Heat through and serve.

The dark meat's flavor penetrates the barley to add a rich taste.

Of all the items on the menu, soup is that which exacts the most delicate perfection and the strictest attention.

— Escoffier

The scent of chicken soup is the first prevention of illness.

Makes 8 servings.
Per Serving: 115 Calories; 2g Fat (18.1% calories from fat); 12g Protein; 12g Carbohydrate; 3g Dietary Fiber; 40mg Cholesterol; 570mg Sodium.

This is a variation from the Bangkok Soup served at the Blue Elephant in London. I just HAD to have a version I could prepare at home.

Scents of Bangkok Soup

- 4 ounces rice noodles, dried
- 8 cups beef broth
- 1 serrano pepper – seeded and minced
- 8 stems cilantro, leaves reserved
- 1/4 teaspoon anise seed
- 1 teaspoon ground pepper
- 2 teaspoons sugar
- 3 Tablespoons fish sauce
- 1/4 cup soy sauce
- 1/3 cup lime juice
- 1/3 cup cilantro – leaves only
- 1/4 cup fresh basil, cut into thin strips
- 2 scallion – thinly sliced
- 2 cups bean sprouts – (or 14 oz. can)
- 3/4 pound steak, thinly sliced
- 1 Tablespoon garlic oil

If using canned bean sprouts, rinse them twice to remove as much salt as possible.

Always cook each item in batches and keep the broth boiling.

1. Place rice noodles in a medium bowl. Cover with cold water and let sit for 20 minutes.
2. In a large stockpot, pour the beef broth, serrano, cilantro stems, anise, and pepper. Bring to a boil.
3. Stir in the sugar, fish sauce, soy sauce and lime juice to the pot, and return to a boil.
4. Divide the cilantro leaves, fresh basil and scallion evenly between six individual bowls.
5. Rinse the bean sprouts and drain. Place bean sprouts in an immersible colander, and submerge in the beef stock for 5 seconds. Divide between the six serving bowls. Return the mixture to a boil.
6. Drain the rice noodles and place in the immersible colander. Submerge in the beef stock for 5 seconds. Divide between the six serving bowls. Return the mixture to a boil.
7. Take four or five pieces of the beef and place in the immersible colander. Submerge in the beef stock for 20 seconds. Divide between the six serving bowls. Repeat until all the beef is cooked.
8. Remove the cilantro stems from the broth. Pour hot broth in each of the bowls. Pour 1/2 teaspoon garlic oil over each bowl and serve immediately with both spoon and fork.

Makes 6 servings.
Per Serving: 328 Calories; 11g Fat (31.1% calories from fat); 25g Protein; 31g Carbohydrate; 2g Dietary Fiber; 33mg Cholesterol; 2428mg Sodium.

What a nice cool change to the standard cold gazpacho soup of the summer!

Cantaloupe-Ricotta Soup

1	large cantaloupe
1 1/2	cups cottage cheese, lowfat
1/2	cup ricotta cheese, part skim milk
2	Tablespoons honey
1	large lime – zested and juiced

1. Slice open the cantaloupe and remove the interior seeds. Using a melon baller, cut 8 pretty pieces from the flesh of the cantaloupe and set aside in the refrigerator. Peel and slice the remaining cantaloupe, and puree in the blender. Pour through a medium strainer, to yield approximately 3 cups of liquid. Discard the remaining pulp of the cantaloupe. Rinse blender.
2. Pour cottage cheese in a medium strainer. Gently turn the cottage cheese over in the strainer a few times to remove the obvious liquid. Measure 1 1/2 cups of the cottage cheese solids and place into the blender. Add the ricotta and blend until very smooth.
3. Add honey, 1 Tablespoon lime juice and cantaloupe juice to the blender and process until smooth. Chill for at least 2 hours.
4. When ready to serve, pour soup into 8 bowls. Garnish with the reserved cantaloupe ball and lime zest

Of course, cantaloupes are always iffy. So, when you taste the soup before chilling it, add 1 extra teaspoon of honey if it isn't quite as sweet as you like. Adding honey instead of sugar keeps the soup from having a gritty taste. Or, if it just needs a little boost, add an extra squeeze of fresh lime just before serving.

Served in china coffee cups, this begins a beautiful brunch.

Makes 8 servings.
Per Serving: 95 Calories; 2g Fat (16.8% calories from fat); 8g Protein; 13g Carbohydrate; 1g Dietary Fiber; 7mg Cholesterol; 198mg Sodium.

Cider-Simmered Squash with Cheddar

Alternately, you could shred all of the cheese. Use half of the quantity to stir into the soup Use the other half to top each bowl and slip under the broiler until it melts and begins to brown.

2 Tablespoons cumin seed – toasted
1/4 cup unsalted butter (1/2 stick)
1 cup onion – diced
3 1/2 pounds butternut squash – peeled and diced
2 quarts apple cider
8 ounces sharp cheddar cheese – (see directions)
1/4 teaspoon cayenne pepper
salt and pepper – to taste

1. In a dry, large soup pot, toast the cumin seeds over medium heat. Stir frequently until they just begin to smell. Melt the butter with the seeds. Add the onion and sauté until soft, 3–5 minutes.
2. Add the squash and cider to the soup pot, and bring to a gentle boil. After about 15 minutes, skim the foam from the top. Boil for a remaining 25–30 minutes until squash is tender.
3. While waiting for the squash to cook, cut the cheddar in half. Using one half, cut into small 1/2 inch cubes, (at least 20). With the other half, grate finely and refrigerate all prepared cheese.
4. When the squash is tender, purée the soup in batches in the blender and return to the pot. [Use caution when blending hot liquids, as the blender top may pop off unexpectedly.] Add cayenne. Gently melt the shredded cheddar into the soup, constantly stirring to avoid lumps. Taste for additional salt and pepper.
5. To serve, ladle into bowls, and toss 2 or more cheddar cheese cubes on top.

Makes 10 servings.
Per Serving: 296 Calories; 13g Fat (37.2% calories from fat); 8g Protein; 41g Carbohydrate; 3g Dietary Fiber; 36mg Cholesterol; 155mg Sodium.

This recipe was the only meatless chili that made the finals for a corporate chili cook-off, in Texas no less!

Souper Bowl Chili

It is possible to make this a day ahead and let the flavors marry; it also freezes well for leftovers.

1	Tablespoon oil
1	teaspoon butter
3	Tablespoons garlic, minced
3	Tablespoons chili powder
3	teaspoons dry mustard
3	teaspoons cumin powder
1 1/2	teaspoons celery seed
1 1/2	teaspoons black pepper
1	teaspoon cayenne pepper
3/4	cup green beans, cut in 1 inch pieces
1 1/2	cups carrot, cut 1/4 inch thick
2	cups celery, cut in 1/2 inch lengths
30	ounces canned tomatoes, chopped
2	cups onion – diced
2	cups bell pepper, cut 1/4 inch x 1 1/2 inch
30	ounces canned kidney beans, save liquid
15	ounces canned hominy, drained
1/2	cup yogurt

1. In a large Dutch oven, heat the oil and butter. Add garlic and dry spices. Sauté over a low flame for about a minute or two. [Note: Adjust cayenne to your liking]
2. Add the green beans, carrots, and celery. Combine juice from the canned tomatoes and water to make 3/4 cup liquid. Stir, then cook covered for about 10 minutes.
3. Add onions and peppers. Cook covered for another 10 minutes.
4. Add the tomatoes, kidney beans with their juice, and hominy. Stir and cook the chili, uncovered, for 10 minutes longer.
5. Taste and add additional salt, if needed. Serve hot with a dollop of fresh yogurt.

Makes 6 servings.
Per Serving: 336 Calories; 6g Fat (16.3% calories from fat); 14g Protein; 60g Carbohydrate; 19g Dietary Fiber; 4mg Cholesterol; 951mg Sodium.

When the season is luring our sweaters out of the closet, we long for satisfying meals that have warmed our hearts.

Rancher's Caldillo with Tamale Puffs

Double acting baking powder works for you twice. The first time is from the addition of liquid, and the second burst of power is from heat. This is why it is added just before use, to get the maximum puff.

- 1 1/2 pounds round steak, cut in 1 1/2 inch cubes
- 3 Tablespoons BBQ Rub mixture – (see recipe index)
- 1 Tablespoon oil
- 1 cup onion – diced
- 15 ounces canned kidney beans
- 14 ounces stewed tomatoes
- 4 ounces green chiles – chopped
- 1 1/2 cups corn – fresh or frozen
- 1 Tablespoon BBQ Rub mixture
- 1/2 cup masa harina
- 1/2 cup cornmeal
- 1 Tablespoon sugar
- 1 1/2 Tablespoons unsalted butter, melted and cooled
- 1 Tablespoon dry milk
- 1 egg white
- 1/3 cup water
- 1 teaspoon baking powder
- 1/4 cup Monterey Pepper Jack cheese, shredded

1. Place diced meat on a large platter and sprinkle with 3 Tablespoons of the Rub mixture.
2. Heat oil in a large Dutch oven. Sauté onions until golden and remove to a bowl.
3. Sear meat on both sides in the Dutch oven, then add back the onions. Stir in kidney beans with juice, stewed tomatoes, chiles, corn, and 1 additional Tablespoon of the Rub mixture. Simmer for 45 minutes or until meat is tender.

This stew travels well when prepared up to the addition of the tamale puffs. It heats up like a champ in a Dutch oven over a campfire, too.

4. In a medium bowl, mix together the masa harina, cornmeal, sugar, butter, dry milk, egg white, and water with a fork. Set aside.
5. About 15 minutes before the stew meat is ready, add the baking powder and cheese to the dry mixture, and blend with a fork. Make small 1/2 inch diameter tamale puff balls with the dough, and float them in the stew the last 10 minutes of cooking time. Dunk them gently into the stew so they can absorb some of the flavors.
6. Ladle stew into bowls and gently place one or two tamale puffs on top.

"I personally didn't care for pork, so to off-set my dislike, I used to imagine them as anything but plain pork chops. After frying the chop to a delicious brown, I would place it on a plate as an island and surround it with snowy mountains of mashed potatoes. I then had a stream of cream gravy around the mountains with bits of parsley on the potatoes as trees. To me, it was a picture created in food, rather than a meal; a genuine 'landscape' dish."

— ***Ebony*** Editor Freda DeKnight, ***A Date with a Dish***

Makes 6 servings.
Per Serving: 499 Calories; 22g Fat (39.1% calories from fat); 32g Protein; 45g Carbohydrate; 6g Dietary Fiber; 80mg Cholesterol; 449mg Sodium.

This soup is a revision of Hadaddah Inselberg's recipe as Winner of the 1990 Jewish Mother's Chicken Soup Festival.

Mother's Golden Chicken Soup

8 ounces skinless chicken breast (about 2 breasts)
1/4 teaspoon Kosher salt
4 sprigs parsley
2 chicken bouillon cubes
1/2 cup turnip, 1/4 inch dice
1/2 teaspoon Kosher salt
8 ounces egg noodles
1 tablespoon olive oil
2 cups zucchini – 1/2 inch dice
3/4 cup carrots – 1/2 inch dice
1/2 cup celery – 1/2 inch dice
1/4 cup scallion – chopped
1/4 cup parsley – chopped
Salt and pepper, to taste

1. Pour 10 cups of water in a large soup pot, and bring to a boil. Add skinned chicken breasts, salt and sprigs of parsley. Boil chicken for 30 minutes.
2. Reduce heat and skim the foam from the top of the broth using paper towels or a large, flat spoon. (Strain broth, if desired.) Reserve chicken and allow to cool. Dice into 1/2 inch pieces and set aside. Take one ladle full of hot broth into a small bowl to dissolve the bouillon cubes. Add back to soup pot with the diced turnip, and additional 1/2 teaspoon salt. Bring soup to a boil over high heat. Add egg noodles and cook 2 minutes short of package directions.
3. While the noodles are cooking, heat oil in a medium skillet. Stir fry the zucchini, carrots, celery and scallion for about 3 minutes. Add the chicken, and continue cooking until chicken begins to have a light golden color. Vegetables will still have a little crunch.
4. Add chicken and vegetable mixture to the large pot. Stir well to marry flavors. After the remaining two minutes for the egg noodles, turn off the heat and stir in the chopped parsley. Taste and season with additional salt and pepper, if necessary. Let stand for 5 minutes before ladling into soup bowls

The egg noodles must have room to expand, as well as have broth for your soup. Be sure you have plenty (at least 8 cups) of broth in the pot when its time to add the egg noodles.

Why is chicken soup the ultimate healer when you are not feeling well? The salt helps you retain those fluids your body needs, and the pasta rests easy on your stomach to help you regain your energy.

Makes 6 servings.
Per Serving: 235 Calories; 5g Fat (18.3% calories from fat); 15g Protein; 34g Carbohydrate; 4g Dietary Fiber; 54mg Cholesterol; 558mg Sodium.

Potato-Bacon Chowder

1	onion, sliced 1/2 inch thick
2	pounds potatoes with skin, sliced 1/8 inch thick
1	teaspoon salt
1	pound bacon slices
3	cups milk
1/2	cup Italian parsley – chopped
1/2	teaspoon ground black pepper

1. Place potatoes and salt in a saucepan and cover with cold water. Cover and bring to boil; remove cover and boil for 10 minutes. Drain.
2. Fry bacon slices in a large cold skillet on medium heat. When bacon is crisp, place slices on paper towels to drain. After it is cool, crumble bacon and set aside.
3. Pour off all but 2 tablespoons bacon fat from the skillet. Sauté onion in bacon fat over medium-high heat for 10 minutes, until soft and golden.
4. Return potatoes to saucepan with the sautéed onions and add milk. Simmer for about 20 minutes until potatoes are fork tender.
5. Add reserved bacon and parsley. Season to taste with freshly ground black pepper.

When frying bacon, start with a cold pan and place the slices snugly together. Do not overlap. When the entire pan starts to bubble, reduce the heat to avoid burning.

Gently break up the potatoes with your spoon as you add the milk and onions.

Makes 4 servings.
Per Serving: 640 Calories; 41g Fat (58.7% calories from fat); 30g Protein; 35g Carbohydrate; 3g Dietary Fiber; 81mg Cholesterol; 1635mg Sodium.

Tieszen Tree Trimmin' Cider
Chile Pecans and Almonds
Texas Gulf Crab Nachos

Feeding The Party Animals

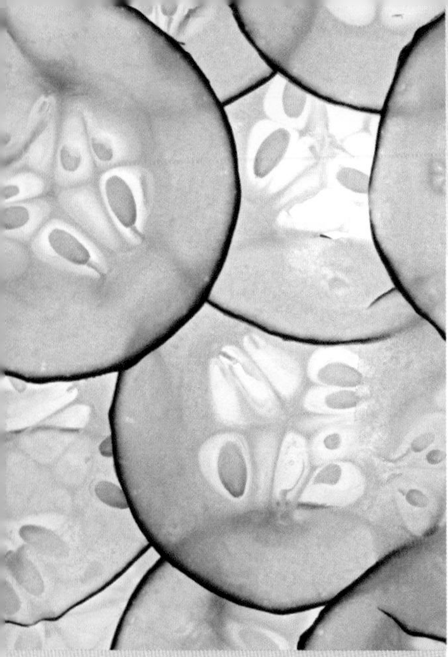

Company Cucumbers

- 3 cucumbers – large
- 1 teaspoon salt
- 1/2 cup yogurt – plain
- 1/2 cup sour cream
- 1/3 cup mayonnaise
- 1 Tablespoon white wine vinegar
- 1/4 cup green onion – chopped
- 1 Tablespoon fresh parsley – minced
- 1 clove garlic – minced
- dash of white pepper

1. Peel cucumbers and slice thin. Place on a large plate and sprinkle with salt. After 15 minutes, pat dry with paper towels and put in serving bowl.
2. In a small bowl, stir together remaining ingredients and mix thoroughly.
3. Pour dressing over cucumbers and toss gently to coat. Refrigerate at least two hours before serving.

The combination of yogurt, sour cream and mayonnaise gives this dressing a very creamy texture. If you are looking to cut calories in this dish, using the light or fat-free varieties will work. For best results, use the thickest light sour cream you can find.

Makes 6 servings.
Per Serving: 163 Calories; 15g Fat (78.9% calories from fat); 3g Protein; 7g Carbohydrate; 1g Dietary Fiber; 15mg Cholesterol; 449mg Sodium.

"To hug a tomato" is the translation from French.

Les Tomates Étreintes

Presto Pesto – prepared as directed, see index
8 crescent rolls – (1 can)
2 Roma tomatoes
16 basil leaves

1. Bring Presto Pesto to room temperature and set aside. Preheat oven to 350F.
2. Lay the crescent rolls out flat, and cut each triangle in half. Spread a slight teaspoon of pesto on each piece, not quite to the edge of the dough.
3. Slice each tomato into 4 wedges. Cut each wedge in half. This will make 16 equal pieces. If you are using non-Roma tomatoes, seed them before slicing.
4. Wrap the tomato slice in a basil leaf, covering the seed/inside portion of the tomato with the widest part of the leaf. Place in the center of the dough, and wrap the corners over the tomato. Pinch to seal, if necessary. Gently place on a baking sheet.
5. Repeat step four with all tomato pieces. Place baking sheet in the oven for 11–15 minutes. These are best when warm and can also be served at room temperature.

I always make more than two per person because folks enjoy these. Prepared pesto in a jar can easily be used.

What now?
If the tomato juice makes the pastry soggy when you take it from the oven, place it on a cooling rack to 'dry out.'

One triangle half will resemble a three cornered hat. Bring each point upward and pinch them together. The other triangle half is elongated and represents the hug on each side of the tomato. (Keep your fingers dry for best results.)

Makes 16 servings.
Per Serving without pesto: 58 Calories; 3g Fat (48.2% calories from fat); 1g Protein; 6g Carbohydrate; trace Dietary Fiber; 0mg Cholesterol; 111mg Sodium.

Just as you must also "Mind the Mead", this may make it difficult "to walka" home.

Tieszen Tree Trimmin' Cider

1	gallon apple cider
1 1/2	cups brown sugar
1	teaspoon nutmeg
2	Tablespoons cinnamon
1	gallon apple cider
750	milliliters Tuaca

1. In a very large stockpot, mix 1 gallon of apple cider with the spices. Heat and stir until all the sugar is dissolved.
2. Add remaining cider and Tuaca. Simmer, stirring occasionally to keep well mixed. Serve very warm.

Each year I invite friends to decorate my fresh-cut East Texas Virginia Pine Tree. I pour this into thermal carafes to serve at the bar. Sparkling Poinsettias (champagne and cranberry juice) are the other holiday drink of choice.

*Coming of Age: You **were** Apple Juice, **now** you're Cider.*

What now?

Why is it listed as 1 gallon twice instead of 2 gallons? I find it hard to stir and completely incorporate the ingredients effectively with that much liquid at once.

Makes 25 servings.
Per Serving: 184 Calories; trace Fat (1.9% calories from fat); trace Protein; 46g Carbohydrate; 1g Dietary Fiber; 0mg Cholesterol; 13mg Sodium.

On Christmas morning, this is served with mini blueberry muffins to tide us over until the extended family meal.

Breakfast Sausage and Egg Bake

16 ounces Italian sausage – spicy
3 cups cheddar cheese – 12 oz. shredded
2 cups Monterey Jack cheese – 8 oz. shredded
2 Tablespoons flour
non-stick spray
8 eggs
1 cup milk, or half-and-half
1 Tablespoon Worcestershire sauce

1. Crumble bulk sausage in a skillet and brown completely. Drain fat; set aside.
2. In a bowl, toss cheeses in flour to coat. Sprinkle cheese mixture in a 13 inch x 9 inch baking dish that has been prepared with a non-stick spray.
3. Beat eggs in a medium bowl. Add milk and Worcestershire, blend well.
4. Arrange cooled, crumbled sausage over cheese mixture. Pour egg mixture over cheese.
5. Cover with plastic wrap and refrigerate for at least six hours or overnight.
6. In the morning, uncover dish and let stand at room temperature for 30 minutes. Preheat oven to 350F. Bake for 45–50 minutes or until egg custard is set when dish is shaken.

I always cover 'overnight' dishes with plastic wrap and write the morning directions on them. That allows anyone to help and not wonder if they bake it 'foil on or off'?

What now?

You ignored the timer, did you? It seems dry when you cut the slices? Put a tablespoon of salsa on the plate and place the slice on top to absorb some of it and add moisture.

For the meatless version, omit the sausage and add two more tablespoons of flour for thickening. Follow the other directions as written.

Makes 12 servings.
Per Serving: 383 Calories; 31g Fat (73.4% calories from fat); 22g Protein; 3g Carbohydrate; trace Dietary Fiber; 219mg Cholesterol; 622mg Sodium.

Herb-Pesto Tray

Yes, ranch-style dressing is always easy, but aren't you ready for a surprise flavor?

1	cup ricotta cheese
1	cup fresh spinach
1 1/2	cups fresh cilantro — or fresh basil
3	cloves garlic — fresh
4	serrano peppers — stemmed
8	ounces goat cheese — fresh, at room temperature
1/4	cup parmesan cheese — freshly grated
2	Tablespoons extra virgin olive oil
	Salt and pepper, to taste
2	pints cherry tomatoes, rinse and dry thoroughly
1	pound snow peas, rinse and trim
2	packages bagel crisps

1. Puree the ricotta cheese, spinach, cilantro (or basil), garlic, and serrano chilies in a blender. Add the goat cheese and parmesan cheese to the blender and pulse on and off a few times to combine. Slowly pour in the olive oil while pulsing blender to make a thick, flowable mixture. Add salt and pepper to taste.
2. Bring 1 quart water to a boil. Add the snow peas and cook 1 minute. Drain and rinse immediately with cold water. Dry thoroughly.
3. Place pesto in a bowl in the center of a large round tray. Arrange vegetables on the tray, leaving space for the bagel crisps. Refrigerate. Add bagel crisps when ready to serve.

For a picnic, place the Herb-Pesto mixture in a resealable bag and place closest to the ice. Other options for vegetables include summer squash, zucchini and cucumbers.

Makes 24 servings.
Per Serving: 94 Calories; 6g Fat (58.8% calories from fat); 6g Protein; 4g Carbohydrate; 1g Dietary Fiber; 16mg Cholesterol; 65mg Sodium.

Tart cranberries find a completely new flavor.

Cranberry Top Hats

- 2 carrots – sliced, at least 3/4 inch diameter
- 1/2 cup water
- 2 Tablespoons anise seed
- 12 ounces fresh cranberries – washed and dried
- 1/2 cup water
- 1/2 cup sugar
- 1 Tablespoon allspice

1. Place carrots, water and anise in a medium saucepan, and cover. Steam until carrots are almost fork tender, about 8–10 minutes. Set aside to cool. Gently brush away most of the anise before assembling the top hats.
2. Place cranberries in a medium flat saucepan where berries make a tight, single layer. In a cup, mix together water, sugar and allspice and pour over the cranberries. Cook uncovered over medium heat for about 3-5 minutes or until cranberries just begin to pop open.
3. To assemble, take one frilled toothpick and pierce a cranberry. Place cranberry on top of a carrot and thread carrot slice to create the 'top hat.' Arrange on a platter.

> *Snow is never more beautiful than in the city. It is wonderful in Paris to stand on a bridge across the Seine looking up through the softly curtaining snow past the gray bulk of the Louvre, up the river spanned by many bridges and bordered by the gray houses of old Paris to where Notre Dame squats in the dusk. You do not know what Christmas is until you lose it in some foreign land.*
>
> —***Christmas in Paris*** by Ernest Hemingway (1899-1961)

Makes 16 servings.
Per Serving: 45 Calories; trace Fat (4.4% calories from fat); trace Protein; 11g Carbohydrate; 2g Dietary Fiber; 0mg Cholesterol; 6mg Sodium.

Summer tomatoes invite you to fill your cheeks with flavor.

Pico De Gallo

To seed a tomato: Cut a tomato in half, place in the palm of your hand, squeeze over the sink and give one quick shake to remove the remaining seeds.

Restaurants usually take the seeded interior of the tomato and add it to whatever broth is simmering in the kitchen using only the outer edge.

- 1 pound red ripe tomatoes, about 4–5 large
- 1 cup onion – finely chopped
- 2 serrano peppers – finely chopped
- 2 cloves garlic – finely minced
- 1 teaspoon salt – to taste
- 1 teaspoon cayenne pepper – to taste
- 1 Tablespoon lemon juice

1. Dice the seeded tomatoes into 1/2 inch pieces and place in a large bowl.
2. Add all other ingredients and toss gently to distribute spices and lemon juice.
3. Let mixture sit for 30 minutes to allow flavors to blend. Give one last stir before serving.

Makes 6 servings.
Per Serving: 28 Calories; trace Fat (9.0% calories from fat); 1g Protein; 6g Carbohydrate; 1g Dietary Fiber; 0mg Cholesterol; 363mg Sodium.

When fully cooked, but not yet cut into squares, this dish can be refrigerated for up to two days. Before serving, cover and heat until warm all the way through.

Jack Cheese and Green Chili Quiche Squares

- 2 whole eggs
- 2 egg whites
- 1/3 cup flour
- 3/4 teaspoon baking powder
- 1 1/2 cups Monterey Jack cheese – shredded
- 1 cup cottage cheese, lowfat
- 4 ounces canned green chiles – diced, drained
- 4 green onions – chopped
- 8 sprigs cilantro – chopped
- Non-stick vegetable cooking spray
- Salsa – for dipping

1. Preheat oven to 350F. In a large bowl, beat eggs and egg whites with electric mixer until fully blended.
2. Combine flour and baking powder and stir to mix well. Add to eggs. Beat with electric mixer to blend well.
3. Add Monterey Jack and cottage cheeses, green chilies, green onions and cilantro. Mix well.
4. Pour mixture into an 11 inch x 7 inch baking pan that has been prepared with a non-stick vegetable cooking spray.
5. Bake for 30 to 35 minutes or until firm and lightly brown on top. Cool in the pan for 10 minutes before cutting into 20 squares.
6. Serve warm with salsa or picante sauce for dipping purposes.

If you double the recipe, it fits nicely in a rimmed cookie sheet or jelly roll pan.

Makes 10 servings.
Per Serving: 121 Calories; 6g Fat (48.3% calories from fat); 10g Protein; 6g Carbohydrate; trace Dietary Fiber; 58mg Cholesterol; 249mg Sodium.

*Happiness doesn't come from having things – it comes from being **part** of things.*

Texas Gulf Crab Nachos

1/2 cup lime juice, fresh
1/4 cup olive oil
3 cloves garlic – minced
1 teaspoon cumin
1/2 teaspoon Kosher salt
1 cup onion, 1/4 inch dice
2 bell peppers, 1/2 inch dice
3 serrano peppers, seeded and finely diced
1 bunch cilantro – stems diced, leaves reserved
6 large tomatoes, 1/2 inch dice
1 pint crab meat – fresh
3 bags tortilla chips, bite-size
4 cups Monterey Jack cheese – shredded
2 cups Colby cheese – or Longhorn, shredded
1/2 cup sour cream

1. Whisk together the lime juice and the olive oil until it is completely incorporated. Add garlic, cumin and salt. Stir briefly and set aside.
2. In a large bowl, gently toss together the onions, both peppers, and cilantro. Pour lime mixture over the vegetables and stir well. Add tomatoes and mix gently. Refrigerate until ready to prepare nachos.
3. Preheat oven to 425F.
4. Arrange chips in one layer on the baking sheets. Drain crabmeat and gently toss into the tomato mixture. Spoon onto chips. Sprinkle with cheese mixture.
5. Bake nachos just until the cheese melts. Dot with sour cream and top with reserved cilantro leaves.

Gentle hands are the key to delectable lump crabmeat.

Makes 30 servings.
Per Serving: 145 Calories; 11g Fat (64.9% calories from fat); 8g Protein; 5g Carbohydrate; 1g Dietary Fiber; 31mg Cholesterol; 209mg Sodium.

I prefer Paul Newman's salad dressings for this recipe. They are full of flavor!

Square Zooks

- 4 large eggs – beaten slightly
- 1/2 cup onion – chopped fine
- 1/2 cup parmesan cheese
- 1/2 cup oil and vinegar salad dressing – (preferably Italian)
- 2 Tablespoons dried oregano
- 1 package biscuit mix, (about 5 ounces)
- 4 cups zucchini – sliced thin

1. Preheat oven to 350F.

2. Beat eggs in a large bowl. Stir in onion, cheese, dressing and oregano. Add biscuit package and mix thoroughly. Add the zucchini to the bowl and make sure it is completely covered with the mixture.

3a. If making as a vegetable side dish, pour batter into an 8 inch x 8 inch glass vegetable dish. Sprinkle a little extra parmesan cheese on top and bake for 40 minutes. Top will be golden brown.

3b. If making as an appetizer, spread a thin layer of the mixture on a non-stick cookie sheet. Spread out the zucchini on the sheet with very little overlap. Sprinkle a little extra parmesan on top and bake for about 25 minutes. Top will be golden brown. Cut into small squares for serving.

"You're not obligated to win. You're obligated to keep trying to do the best you can everyday."

—Marian Wright Edelman,
Roar Softly and Carry a Great Lipstick

Makes 48 servings.
Per Serving: 35 Calories; 2g Fat (60.6% calories from fat); 1g Protein; 2g Carbohydrate; trace Dietary Fiber; 18mg Cholesterol; 54mg Sodium.

Chile Pecans and Almonds

- 2 Tablespoons butter
- 1 1/2 cups pecan halves
- 1 1/2 cups whole almonds
- 1/2 cup light brown sugar
- 1 teaspoon paprika
- 2 teaspoons chili powder – ancho or chipotle
- 1 Tablespoon cumin
- 1/4 cup apple cider vinegar
- Seasoned salt, to taste

1. Preheat oven to 350F.
2. In a large skillet melt butter over medium high heat. Stir in the nuts and sauté until lightly browned, about two to three minutes.
3. Add brown sugar to the pan and cook until the nuts are lightly caramelized.
4. Stir in the paprika, chile powder and cumin. Shield your face as you pour the vinegar in the pan. Its important to continuously stir until all the liquid has evaporated. This will prevent the nuts from clinging together.
5. Spread the nut mixture into a single layer on a foil lined baking sheet. Bake until crisp, about three to five minutes. Sprinkle with seasoned salt just as they are removed from the oven. When cool, keep in an airtight container.

I encourage holding your breath preparing for the pungent cloud that accompanies the addition of the vinegar. It's a necessary evil to seal the coating to the nuts.

For an adventure, try ancho chile powder or chipotle chile powder.

What now?

Nuts don't taste any better burned with sugar. Pick out the bad ones, or simply start over.

Makes 12 servings.
Per Serving: 239 Calories; 20g Fat (72.4% calories from fat); 5g Protein; 13g Carbohydrate; 3g Dietary Fiber; 5mg Cholesterol; 29mg Sodium.

The unusually cut shapes and delightful flavors make this appetizer a hit!

Marvelous Muffaletta

30 ounces pimento stuffed olives – drained
15 ounces garbanzo beans, canned – drained
14 ounces artichoke hearts – drained
16 ounces marinated vegetables – jarred
2 stalks celery – cut in large chunks
2 bell peppers – cut in large chunks
1 Tablespoon capers
4 ounces pimientos
3 cloves garlic – minced
1 Tablespoon fresh basil
1 Tablespoon fresh oregano
1 large pizza crust – prepared
2 cups Monterey Jack cheese – or pepper jack, shredded

1. In a large food processor, combine drained olives, garbanzo beans, and artichoke hearts. Pulse a few times until ingredients are slightly chopped.
2. Drain and reserve the liquid from the marinated vegetables. Add marinated vegetables, celery, bell pepper, capers and pimentos to the food processor. Pulse on and off until mixture is chunky and well blended.
3. Transfer mixture to a large bowl. Using a long handled spatula, fold in the minced garlic and dried spices. Add marinated vegetable liquid, one Tablespoon at a time, if the mixture appears dry. Muffaletta should be moist to the touch, but not mushy.
4. Spread the muffaletta mixture on a prepared pizza crust. Layer cheese over the muffaletta. Place under a hot broiler just until the cheese melts and starts to bubble. Slice into diamond shapes and arrange on a platter to serve.

As a sandwich, this travels as easily to a tailgate as to a non-profit board meeting. Add potato chips and a fruit salad to make a complete meal.

What now?

Too wet? Let the mixture sit in a strainer for 10–15 minutes, stir and sit 5 minutes more.

To make a large Muffaletta Sandwich, spread spicy mustard, or a vinegar and oil based Italian dressing on a large french loaf. Make two sets of layers of meat, muffaletta and cheese using any combination of turkey, ham, salami, pastrami and provolone, Monterey Jack cheese, Swiss cheese, ending with the cheese layer. Put under broiler just until the cheese melts and starts to bubble. Serve warm. If traveling with the sandwich, slide gently back into the foil bread sack and slice when you arrive. Makes about 8–10 servings.

Makes 20 servings.
Per Serving (Without Bread): 209 Calories; 8g Fat (31.9% calories from fat); 10g Protein; 27g Carbohydrate; 5g Dietary Fiber; 10mg Cholesterol; 962mg Sodium.

Apple Pizza
Yogurt Yummies
Teddy Bear Sandwiches

Kid's Collection

This is great as a Mother's or Father's day breakfast, when an adult helps with the apples and the microwave.

What now?
Are those pancake wedges not cooperating to look 'pretty'? Scoop the wedge into a large coffee cup and serve with a long handled spoon.

Quick Apple Pancakes

1/4 cup unsalted butter – melted, (1/2 stick)
1/2 cup sugar
1/2 teaspoon cinnamon
1/2 teaspoon nutmeg
4 apples – peeled, thinly sliced

1 package pancake mix, complete – about 6 ounces
1/2 teaspoon cinnamon
1/4 teaspoon nutmeg
1 cup water
1 teaspoon vanilla
2 Tablespoons sugar
1/2 teaspoon cinnamon

1. Stir together the melted butter, sugar, cinnamon and nutmeg. Layer the apples in a 9 inch glass pie plate. Pour the butter mixture over the apples to coat. Cover with wax paper and microwave on high for 3 to 4 minutes or until apples are tender.
2. In medium bowl, blend all batter ingredients: pancake mix, cinnamon, nutmeg, water, and vanilla. Pour evenly over cooked apples.
3. In small bowl, combine the sugar and cinnamon with a fork; sprinkle over batter. Microwave on high for 3 to 5 minutes or until a toothpick inserted 2 inches from the edge comes out clean. Let stand for 5 minutes.
4. Cut into wedges. Flip wedges upside down on the plate when serving.

If serving as a dessert, top with ice cream, or non-dairy whipped topping.

Makes 6 servings.
Per Serving: 289 Calories; 9g Fat (27.8% calories from fat); 2g Protein; 51g Carbohydrate; 3g Dietary Fiber; 25mg Cholesterol; 266mg Sodium.

Eat now. Re-heat later. Take with you. I love options!

Soccer Practice Supper

1	pound lean ground beef
1	egg
1	cup onion, cut in 1/4 inch pieces
3/4	cup cornmeal
1	Tablespoon chili powder
1	Tablespoon cumin
1	Tablespoon oregano
1	garlic clove – minced
2	teaspoons red pepper flakes
8	cheese sticks
16	ounces tomato sauce
1	Tablespoon chili powder
1	package hot dog buns

1. In a large bowl, place beef, egg, onions, cornmeal, chili powder, cumin, oregano, garlic and red pepper flakes. Mix thoroughly by hand.
2. Spoon out approximately 2/3 cup of meat. Form the meat mixture around the cheese stick, into a shape that will fit easily in a hot dog bun. Be sure the cheese is completely sealed by the meat to prevent burning.
3. In a large frying pan, add the meat dogs in one layer, and brown gently on all sides. While the meat is browning, pour the tomato sauce into a bowl and mix with the 1 Tablespoon of chili powder. Pour over meat and cover.
4. Lower heat and simmer meat dogs for about 15 minutes. Serve in hot dog buns for a quick table meal, or an on-the-go dinner.

"... his very own room where he found his supper waiting for him, and it was still hot."

— ***Where the Wild Things Are***, Maurice Sendak

What now?
Too spicy for younger ones? Omit the red pepper flakes and the chili powder from the sauce.

Makes 8 servings.
Per Serving: 377 Calories; 23g Fat (56.8% calories from fat); 20g Protein; 20g Carbohydrate; 3g Dietary Fiber; 99mg Cholesterol; 622mg Sodium.

An edible birthday party centerpiece.

ROOOOOOARRRRR

T-Rex Tall

12 cups popcorn, air-popped
1 cup sugar
1/3 cup light corn syrup
1/3 cup water
1/4 cup butter – (1/2 stick)
1 teaspoon salt
1 teaspoon vanilla
1 teaspoon green food coloring

15 wheat crackers, 1/2 inch square
20 pieces candy corn
2 M&Ms™ with peanuts chocolate candy – red
peanut butter – (optional)

1. Line a large tray with wax paper, or cover a large work surface. Put popcorn into a bowl large enough for mixing.
2. Mix the sugar, corn syrup, water, butter, and salt into a 2 quart saucepan. Cook to the hard-crack stage on a candy thermometer, about 300F. Add food coloring and vanilla to make the perfect dinosaur color.
3. Pour the mixture over popcorn in the large bowl. Wearing plastic gloves, mix and quickly shape the following pieces from the popcorn: body and tail, head with an open jaw, 2 arms and 2 legs. If a few of you work quickly, the pieces can be connected by the syrup mixture. The body parts are more secure when using toothpicks to attach the head, arms and legs. (Be sure to warn your human predators)
4. Using the wheat squares, wedge them into the back of the dinosaur to make scales. Using the candy corn points, make fierce teeth in the jaws. Using the two red M&Ms, place the eyes on the head. If the popcorn mixture has cooled too much to attach these, use peanut butter as 'glue.'

"What do you like doing best in the world, Pooh?" asked Christopher Robin. "Well," said Pooh, "What I like best ..." What do we call that moment just before we begin to eat the honey?

— ***The Tao of Pooh*** by Benjamin Hoff

Makes 6 servings.
Per Serving: 371 Calories; 10g Fat (23.4% calories from fat); 3g Protein; 70g Carbohydrate; 3g Dietary Fiber; trace Cholesterol; 543mg Sodium.

Long carrot stick 'fishing poles' make this a great lunch catch!

Fisherman's Pockets

1	medium onion – chopped
1/2	cup mayonnaise
2	teaspoons pepper
1	teaspoon salt
12	ounces tuna in water – drained
16	ounces coleslaw – packaged
4	rounds whole wheat pita bread – cut in half

1. In a large bowl, mix the chopped onion. mayonnaise, pepper, salt and tuna until well blended.
2. Add the coleslaw into the tuna mixture. Blend well and cover with plastic wrap. Refrigerate for at least 15 minutes.
3. Gently open the pita bread to stuff the pockets. If there is liquid in the bottom of the tuna bowl, drain it before continuing. Spoon tuna into the pitas and enjoy.

This mixture easily transports for a picnic – maybe even onto the fishing boat!

In the 16th century, when Charles IX decreed Jan 1st as New Year's Day, rather than the traditional April 1st (Solstice), the French April Fool's Day traditions began. Those who didn't follow the new calendar were called "fools" and sent invitations to fake parties. French children would fool their friends by taping a paper fish to their friends' backs – then when discovered, the child yells "Poisson d'avril!"

Makes 4 servings.
Per Serving: 557 Calories; 29g Fat (44.0% calories from fat); 30g Protein; 52g Carbohydrate; 7g Dietary Fiber; 44mg Cholesterol; 1345mg Sodium.

Breakfast Pudding To Go

- 2 cups instant oatmeal
- 6 dashes cinnamon
- 6 Tablespoons raisins – (3 single serving boxes)
- 1 package vanilla pudding mix – non-instant
- 3 cups 1% low-fat milk
- 3/4 cup unsweetened applesauce

1. In each of 6 coffee mugs, mix 1/3 cup uncooked oatmeal, 1 dash cinnamon, and 1 Tablespoon raisins. Stir to combine.
2. Cook pudding to package directions. (You can use skim milk to reduce the fat content.)
3. Pour 1/2 cup of cooked pudding into each mug and stir immediately. This will "cook" the oatmeal.
4. Spoon 2 Tablespoons of applesauce over each pudding and spread to just cover the top.
5. Serve immediately, or cover with plastic wrap and refrigerate.

Sliced peaches are a good option on top in place of the applesauce.

Microwave refrigerated pudding for about a minute for an on-the-go breakfast in a handy coffee mug!

Makes 6 servings.
Per Serving: 252 Calories; 3g Fat (10.8% calories from fat); 9g Protein; 49g Carbohydrate; 4g Dietary Fiber; 5mg Cholesterol; 574mg Sodium.

Teddy Bear Sandwiches

The highlight of my childhood was making my brother laugh so hard that food came out his nose.

—Garrison Keillor

Almost any spreadable sandwich filling can go into this Teddy's tummy.

1	package active dry yeast
1/2	teaspoon salt
2	Tablespoons sugar
1 1/2	cups whole-grain wheat flour
1	cup water, lukewarm, 110F
3	Tablespoons honey
3	Tablespoons unsalted butter
1/4	cup water, very warm, 120F–150F
2 1/2	cups all-purpose flour
12	ounces canned chicken – drained
1/2	cup celery, cut in 1/4 inch pieces
1/4	cup mayonnaise
1	large apple, cut in 1/2 inch pieces
20	grapes – cut in quarters

1. Preheat oven to 350F.
2. Mix yeast, salt, sugar and wheat flour together with a fork until ingredients are well incorporated. Pour in 1/4 cup very warm water and beat until smooth. Add honey, butter and hot water to the dough. Combine up to 2 cups of all-purpose flour to create a soft, workable dough. Cover with a towel; set in warm place for approximately an hour or until doubled in bulk.
3. Turn out onto floured surface, mix in up to 1/2 cup of all-purpose flour, and knead until smooth and elastic, about 2–3 minutes. Add additional flour by Tablespoonfuls if dough begins to get sticky.
4. Using a pastry scraper or dull knife, cut dough into 16 equal pieces. Shape 8 of the pieces into an oval for the body, and a ball for the head. Make smaller balls of dough from the remaining pieces for the ears, arms, legs, and nose.
5. Using a large spatula, place shaped teddy bears on lightly greased cookie sheets and place in oven for 20 minutes until golden brown. Remove to racks for cooling to keep bread from becoming soggy on the bottom. When ready to serve, slice the teddy bears lengthwise into two large sandwich bread pieces, and follow the inset directions.

Filling:

1. Drain chicken and place in mixing bowl. Add celery and mix to combine.
2. Mix the mayonnaise with the apple quickly after cutting to keep the apple from turning brown. Combine with grapes and add to chicken mixture.
3. Stir gently. Refrigerate until ready to serve.

Makes 8 servings.
Per Serving: 430 Calories; 14g Fat (29.7% calories from fat); 17g Protein; 60g Carbohydrate; 5g Dietary Fiber; 40mg Cholesterol; 397mg Sodium.

If the world was crazy,
you know what I'd eat?
A big slice of soup and
a whole quart of meat,
A lemonade sandwich,
and then I might try
Some roasted ice
cream or a bicycle pie.

— **Where the Sidewalk Ends**
by Shel Silverstein

When the kids gather for this, don't let on it's a science experiment … gone yummy.

To serve this cake (if desired), slice and remove small sections where the lava mixture was absorbed by the angel food cake. The rest of the mountain is yours!

Mt. Vesuvius Volcano Cake

1 angel food cake — (prepared)
12 ounces chocolate frosting — (prepared)
1/2 cup chocolate wafer cookies — crushed
1 tube Green Gel icing

2 packets gelatin powder — plain
1/2 cup water — cool
1/2 cup water — boiling
1/2 teaspoon red food coloring
2 drops green food coloring
2 ounces lemon juice
1 Tablespoon baking soda
1 teaspoon water

1. Open packaged angel food cake and place on rimmed plate. Find a juice glass that will slide easily about halfway down the opening in the middle, where the top of the glass won't show over the top of the cake. Set aside.
2. Using chocolate frosting, cover the angel food cake. Add "dirt and mud" with the crushed cookies. Using the green gel icing, add a bit of "grass" and other "vegetation." When the icing is complete, assemble the ingredients for the "lava."
3. In a small bowl, sprinkle the gelatin over 1/2 cup of cool water. Let stand for 1 minute.
4. Add the boiling water and stir up to 3 minutes to dissolve the gelatin. Add the red and green food coloring to make dark red lava.
5. Fill the "lava pit" glass halfway up with the warm gelatin mixture. Add the lemon juice to reach about 1/2 inch from the top of the glass. Slide gently into the "mouth" of the volcano. Push down so that no sides of the glass will show.
6. In a small glass, mix the baking soda with 1 teaspoon of water to make a thick pourable mixture.
7. Place the volcano where you are prepared for the fun. Quickly pour the baking soda mixture into the mouth of the volcano and stand back for the dramatic lava flow.

Makes 12 servings.
Per Serving: 338 Calories; 6g Fat (16.8% calories from fat); 5g Protein; 67g Carbohydrate; 1g Dietary Fiber; trace Cholesterol; 713mg Sodium.

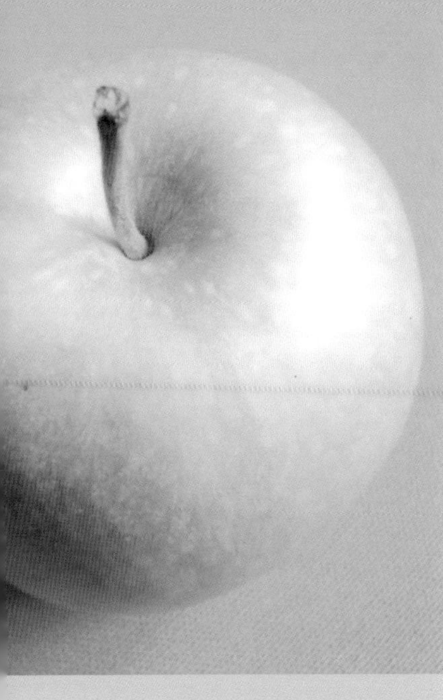

Apple Pizza

1	can pizza dough
2	Tablespoons sugar
5	apples
1/2	cup water
1	teaspoon lemon juice
1/2	cup sugar
3	Tablespoons cinnamon
1/4	cup mozzarella cheese – or queso fresco

1. Preheat oven to 350F. Prepare a baking sheet or pizza pan with non-stick spray.
2. Roll out the pizza crust into desired shape. Place on baking sheet and sprinkle lightly with 2 tablespoons of sugar.
3. Core and peel the apples. Slice thinly to make about 16 or more long slices per apple.
4. In a very large skillet, pack the apple pieces as flat as possible. Gently pour in the water and lemon juice. Simmer the apples until almost all the water has evaporated.
5. Add the sugar and cinnamon to the apples and toss to coat. Place them in an overlapping pattern on the pizza crust.
6. Sprinkle the cheese over the apples.
7. Bake for 15 minutes, or until golden brown. Slice like a pizza and serve.

Apple varieties to use include Granny Smith and Golden or Red Delicious.

[Part 1 of 2: From an American expatriate web log; permission granted from Princess Gwenniel]

American kids are easy to feed; especially children in my family, whose gastronomical tastes tend to lean toward anything fried to a crisp or boiled beyond recognition in a tub of pig fat. An outing to the drive-thru was considered fine dining. On those rare occasions in which the children would be invited to a dinner party (complete with paper napkins), they would gleefully accept a steaming plate of sautéed grass topped with a splash of twigs, and think to themselves, "Ah, now that's good eatin'!"

I have never been gifted in the food arts, but I know a good meal when one accidentally drops on my palette. Whenever I had to cook for American children, I could always take comfort in the fact that their little stomachs were already used to anything, so it didn't matter if I fed them old shoes laced with tomato sauce and sprinkled with toe cheese. [Continued …]

Makes 8 servings.
Per Serving: 226 Calories; 2g Fat (9.1% calories from fat); 4g Protein; 50g Carbohydrate; 4g Dietary Fiber; 3mg Cholesterol; 17mg Sodium.

Even the youngest chef can make these.

Blueberry Brights for Kids

1	pint blueberries
2	tablespoons flour
2	cups flour, all-purpose
1/2	cup sugar
2	teaspoons baking powder
1/2	teaspoon salt
1	egg – beaten
1/3	cup oil
1	cup milk

1. Rinse and check blueberries. Toss with the 2 Tablespoons of flour. Set aside. Preheat oven to 350F.
2. Carefully measure the flour, sugar, baking powder, and salt into a large bowl. Remember to let air into the flour. Mix thoroughly with a fork.
3. Break egg into a small bowl. (Check for shells.) Beat egg lightly with fork.
4. Measure oil, and pour into bowl with egg. Mix with fork.
5. Measure milk, and add to wet mixture. Mix together with fork.
6. Using a spatula, make a volcano hole in the middle of the flour mixture.
7. Pour the wet ingedients mixture into the volcano to create the lava overflow.
8. Mix gently with fork, then use spatula as the mixture get a little harder to mix. (Remember: gently, not to create anthills in the muffins.)
9. Sprinkle blueberries over the batter. Slide the spatula into the batter in the 3 o'clock position, turn it over gently when you get to the center of the bowl, and come out at the 6 o'clock position. Next, do it again, going from 12 o'clock to 3 o'clock. Then one more time from the 9 o'clock to 12 o'clock position to mix the blueberries with the batter.
10. Spoon into paper-lined muffin tins. (Wipe the drips.) Bake for 25 minutes.

Makes 12 servings.
Per Serving: 199 Calories; 7g Fat (33.4% calories from fat); 4g Protein; 30g Carbohydrate; 1g Dietary Fiber; 20mg Cholesterol; 188mg Sodium.

Yogurt Yummies

2 cups strawberries – one green pint basket
2 cups blackberries – one green pint basket
1/2 cup sugar
32 ounces plain low-fat yogurt – (or 4–8 oz. containers)

1. Rinse and pick over the fruit. Stem and slice strawberries. Cut large blackberries in half. Put fruit in a large bowl, sprinkle with sugar and stir. Set aside for 5 minutes.
2. Pour yogurt over the fruit, and stir gently. Serve in small glass bowls. If using 8 ounce yogurt cups, spoon some of the mixture back into the containers, cover and freeze for a snack later.

A 10–12 oz. bag of frozen fruit also works well when fresh fruit isn't in season. Thaw slightly on paper towels to absorb the excess moisture so your yogurt stays creamy.

| Part 2 of 2: From an American expatriate web log; permission granted from Princess Gwenniel

My lunch responsibilities today include two Swedish children. I'm not sure about the visiting kid, but my young friend is just eleven years old with very grown up taste. The product of a Swedish mother and a French father – this little kid is used to good food. Here in Belgium, she's been exposed to some really classy food joints. This is the type of little girl who would order a filet mignon so rare, that the sizzle on the plate would be preceded by "moo," followed by the blast of pneumatic hammers. Waiters would stand in silent anguish as she swirled her glass of Orangina … paused … inhaled its effervescence, and then gave the nod of approval.

Today, when left with the responsibility of making lunch for two Swedish children, a fragrance of gloom wafted into the kitchen. I was sitting in my room practicing some French when the girls appeared and said, "We are hungry." Here was my big chance to make an impression. "What could I make them?" I thought. Perhaps chicken cordon bleu? Quiche Lorraine? Steak tartare? Oh, blast. What's French for "food poisoning?"

There I was, surrounded by an army of pots boiling with just water. Now, all I have to do is put food in them and everything will be okay, right? I prayed – not to God, but to the spirit of Julia Child. "Please merciful Julia, let me make these children a fine meal, let them be satisfied and happy. Bless them, oh Julia, so that I will not have to call their parents and explain "intestinal maladie" in my poor disgraceful French. Bless this kitchen, so that I will not burn down the house. And please dear Julia, give me the knowledge to understand the French phrases for "this food sucks," and "feed this to the cats!"

As I knelt down praying to Julia, I heard her whisper "Pasta, my child. And the left over chicken from last night!!" Thank you dear Julia! So, there you have it. I set the table with the style of an English butler. Everything was in place; cloth napkins, candles, soft music, and flowers. The food was presented to them, and as I left the room, there was the sound of girlish giggles and the tinkle of forks hitting the plates.

Makes 6 servings.
Per Serving: 200 Calories; 3g Fat (11.8% calories from fat); 9g Protein; 37g Carbohydrate; 4g Dietary Fiber; 9mg Cholesterol; 107mg Sodium.

Miel Madeleines
Gâteau Carotte D'Oliveira
Gelato Ravioli with Strawberry Purée
Gingersnaps, Initially Yours

Sweet On You

Single layer cakes are popular in France for a touch of sweetness following a multi-course meal.

Chocolate Génoise

1/3	cup cake flour
1/3	cup cornstarch
1/4	cup cocoa powder
1/4	teaspoon baking soda
3	eggs
3	egg yolks
3/4	cup sugar
1/4	teaspoon salt
4	ounces non-dairy whipped topping
1/2	cup miniature chocolate chips – or chocolate curls

1. Preheat oven to 350F. Line a 9 inch round cake pan with parchment paper. Allow the paper to come about halfway up the sides. Press firmly into the pan for a tight fit.
2. Start a pot of water simmering on the stove. The pot should be slightly larger than the mixing bowl.
3. Combine the cake flour, cornstarch, cocoa powder and baking soda into a small bowl and blend with a fork.
4. In an electric mixer, whisk the whole eggs and egg yolks. While the mixer is running, slowly add the sugar and salt.
5. Place the mixing bowl over a pan of simmering water and gently whisk until the egg mixture is warm to the touch. Remove bowl from heat. Mix on high speed until the egg mixture cools and increases in volume.
6. Remove the bowl from the mixer and sift about 1/3 of the cake flour blend over the egg mixture. Fold in with a rubber spatula. Repeat twice with the remaining flour blend. Pour the batter into the prepared pan and smooth the top evenly with the spatula.
7. Bake the layer for about 25 minutes, until well risen and firm to the touch.
8. Loosen the layer from the sides of the pan with a knife and invert to a wire cooling rack; immediately re-invert to the rack so that the cake layer cools on the paper. When fully cooled, cover the cake with non-dairy whipped topping. Sprinkle miniature chocolate chips or curls across the top. Refrigerate or serve immediately.

Of course you can use real whipping cream!

This cake can be made gluten-free by substituting 3 Tablespoons of white rice flour and 2 Tablespoons of chestnut flour for the cake flour. Verify the cocoa powder is also gluten-free by contacting the manufacturer.

Makes 12 servings.
Per Serving: 145 Calories; 5g Fat (22.1% calories from fat); 3g Protein; 24g Carbohydrate; 1g Dietary Fiber; 106mg Cholesterol; 96mg Sodium.

Growing up, one of our neighbors made the most delicious toffee. My mother's bridge friends loved every bite.

Top-Notch Toffee

- 1/2 cup pecans — toasted and ground
- 1 cup unsalted butter — (2 sticks)
- 3/4 cup granulated sugar
- 1/2 cup light brown sugar — packed
- 1/4 cup water
- 1/8 teaspoon cream of tartar
- 1/2 cup chocolate — roughly chopped
- 1/4 cup pecans — toasted (optional)

1. Prepare a 13 inch x 9 inch pan with non-stick spray, and sprinkle pecans in the bottom.
2. In a 2 quart saucepan, slowly melt butter. Add sugars, water and cream of tartar. Bring to a boil, stirring constantly. Boil for approximately 5–7 minutes until the candy reaches the hard-ball stage (260F on a candy thermometer).
3. Quickly pour toffee into the dish as evenly as possible. It will be thick and will not spread easily once it cools.
4. Sprinkle the chopped chocolate over the toffee and use a knife to spread it as it melts. If desired, sprinkle the additional 1/4 cup of pecans over the melted chocolate.
5. Allow toffee to cool for about 15 minutes. Use a knife handle to break the toffee into pieces. Put in airtight containers.

Makes 24 servings.
Per Serving: 269 Calories; 20g Fat (61% calories from fat); 1g Protein; 27g Carbohydrate; 2g Dietary Fiber; 21mg Cholesterol; 7mg Sodium.

*The long stemmed strawberry gives the most **beautiful** kiss.*

Strawberry Kissed Croissant Bread Pudding

If the packaged croissants are very moist or buttery they may not need all of the liquid. Heat the remaining liquid to a gentle boil to thicken. Serve on the plates under the bread pudding.

If the cholesterol in this recipe is past your limit, try these substitutions: 6 egg substitute portions, 1 cup whole milk (instead of cream) plus 2 cups skim milk. As for the chocolate, 1/4 inch square caramel pieces are an option.

12 croissants — torn in pieces
12 ounces chocolate — cut in 1/2 inch pieces
1 cup heavy cream
1 Tablespoon vanilla extract
1 cup sugar
3 large eggs
3 egg yolks
2 cups milk
12 strawberries — with stems

1. Preheat the oven to 350F. Prepare a non-metallic 13 inch x 9 inch pan with non-stick spray.
2. Place most of the torn croissants in the prepared pan. Tuck and hide the chocolate pieces among the croissants. Cover about half of the chocolate with the remaining croissant pieces.
3. Heat the cream in a glass measuring cup in the microwave for 1 minute. Stir in the vanilla and heat one minute more.
4. Whisk together the sugar, eggs and egg yolks in a medium bowl. Slowly add the warm vanilla cream and whisk to combine. Stir in the milk to incorporate thoroughly.
5. Pour the egg mixture through a small strainer over the croissants. When half of the liquid has been poured, gently push down the bread with the back of a soup spoon to encourage absorption of the cream. Pour remaining liquid over the bread pudding.
6. Place the 13 x 9 in a slightly larger pan, and pour hot water in the larger pan to a depth of about 1 inch. [Officially known as a bain-marie]. A lipped cookie sheet or jelly roll pan works well.
7. Bake in the pre-heated oven for about 45 minutes and until a knife comes out wet, but clear.
8. Slice into squares, and top with the strawberry on each plate.

Makes 12 servings.
Per Serving: 573 Calories; 33g Fat (50.3% calories from fat); 10g Protein; 63g Carbohydrate; 3g Dietary Fiber; 177mg Cholesterol; 476mg Sodium.

Serve on top of a small flat scoop of ice cream for a spin on the traditional apple pie preparation: "Pomme l'envers à la mode"

Deux à Duet

- 4 large apples – Jonagold or Gala
- 4 Tablespoons dried apricot halves – 1/4 inch dice
- 2 Tablespoons orange juice
- 1 Tablespoon honey
- 1 teaspoon anise seed
- 1 teaspoon orange zest
- 1 Tablespoon Triple sec – optional

1. Preheat oven to 350F. Rinse apples and pat dry.
2. Core apples, being careful not to pierce the bottom core covering, as it is needed to hold the filling.
3. Place remaining ingredients in a small bowl and mix thoroughly to combine. Divide evenly between the 4 apples and spoon into the open core.
4. Put apples in a glass or ceramic dish and place in oven for 20 minutes. The interior of the apple will give easily to a fork when the apple is cooked through.

These days, the late summer flowers, the first fall of a few leaves, the earlier sunsets, all remind me that autumn is delicious; a crisp memory of summer gone that tastes like a tart apple straight from the tree.

— From a web food blog

Makes 4 servings.
Per Serving: 152 Calories; 1g Fat (3.6% calories from fat); 1g Protein; 37g Carbohydrate; 5g Dietary Fiber; 0mg Cholesterol; 2mg Sodium.

Frequently requested as a groom's cake. This is festive for any everyday occasion.

Chocolate "Quiet as a Mousse" Cake

12 ounces semisweet chocolate
1 cup butter — (2 sticks)
5 eggs — separated
1/4 cup raspberry liqueur — or Crème de Cassis
1/2 cup sugar
3/4 cup heavy cream
1 teaspoon vanilla
1/2 cup chocolate curls

1. Preheat oven to 350F. Grease and flour a springform pan.
2. In a double boiler over simmering water, melt the chocolate with the butter. Transfer to a mixing bowl, and cool to room temperature.
3. Add the egg yolks and liqueur to the chocolate, and stir to mix. In a separate bowl, beat the egg whites to soft peaks. Continue beating, and slowly add the sugar.
4. Whisk a small portion of the whites into the chocolate mixture to lighten it. Fold in the remaining whites. Pour 2/3 of the batter into the springform pan, and bake for 20 minutes.
5. Whip the cream with the vanilla until stiff. Fold it into the remaining batter, creating mousse. Refrigerate.
6. Allow the cake to cool for 30 minutes at room temperature. Remove cake from the pan by running a knife around the sides. Inserting a long metal spatula underneath the cake, gently pry from the pan. Handle very carefully as the cake crumbles easily.
7. Frost the cake with the chocolate mousse, and decorate with chocolate curls. Refrigerate for two hours before serving.

Alternately, the batter mixture (without cream) can be evenly divided between two prepared springform pans and frosted with the ganache on the following page.

[Warning: Raw eggs may contain harmful bacteria known to cause serious illness. Small children, the elderly or people with compromised immune systems are more susceptible.]

Makes 12 servings.
Per Serving: 688 Calories; 51g Fat (62.4% calories from fat); 6g Protein; 62g Carbohydrate; 3g Dietary Fiber; 150mg Cholesterol; 203mg Sodium.

Seriously chocolate frosting. Seriously chocolate. Seriously.

Ganache

1 1/2	cups heavy cream
1/3	cup light corn syrup
24	ounces bittersweet chocolate – (65% or higher)
5	Tablespoons unsalted butter – softened
1	Tablespoon brandy – optional

1. In a medium saucepan, combine the cream and corn syrup. Place over medium heat and bring to a boil. Remove from heat and add the chocolate and butter. Allow to stand for 3–4 minutes, then whisk smooth. Add liqueur and whisk, if using.
2. Scrape the frosting from the pan to a bowl to cool and thicken. To use immediately, stir it over a bowl of ice until cooled and of spreading consistency. Alternately, refrigerate and bring back to room temperature to spread. (It is not recommended to place in the freezer.) Stir to lighten before using. Thoroughly chill the cake to set the frosting prior to serving.

A very high quality chocolate such as Scharffen-Berger, Green & Black's organic, or Lindt is recommended.

Why did God or Darwin, or whatever other force was responsible for stirring up the universe give us the blustery realities of February, and then — to tease us — stick the oasis of Valentine's Day smack in its heart? February is supposed to be terrible and gloomy, filled with wintry depression and light-deprived despair. The chocolate-deranged among us know the answer: the middle of February is our supply ship steaming in over the wind-wracked sea, its confectioned provisions packed neatly into boxes and tied up with bows.

—***On Chocolate Love and War*** by Jeff Silverman

Makes 12 servings.
Per Serving: 469 Calories; 47g Fat (77.8% calories from fat); 6g Protein; 24g Carbohydrate; 9g Dietary Fiber; 54mg Cholesterol; 31mg Sodium.

Fresh fruit flavors of summer, on ice.

Pluot Sorbet (Plum-Apricot)

- 2/3 cup water
- 2/3 cup sugar
- 8 pluots – peeled and chopped
- 2 Tablespoons lime juice – (1/2 lime)
- 2 Tablespoons vodka – optional
- 6 mint leaves
- 6 toothpicks

1. Create a simple syrup with the water and sugar. Bring the water to a boil in a microwave. Stir in the sugar to dissolve. Refrigerate the simple syrup until it is cold, or freeze for about 10 minutes while you prepare the fruit.
2. Pour the lime juice, vodka and chopped fruit into the blender. Blend for about 30 seconds. Add the simple syrup and process until smooth.
3. Place the mixture in the container of an ice cream maker, and follow manufacturer's directions. Alternately, soft freeze the mixture in an ice cube tray.
4. Using a toothpick, pierce the top and bottom of a mint leaf to create a small sail.
5. In a small bowl, scoop approximately 1/4 to 1/3 cup of sorbet, and garnish with a mint leaf sail.

A blend of red and black plums can also be used if pluots are out of season or difficult to find at your local grocer.

Makes 6 servings.
Per Serving: 147 Calories; 1g Fat (0.0% calories from fat); 1g Protein; 34g Carbohydrate; 1g Dietary Fiber; 0mg Cholesterol; 1mg Sodium.

Alphabetic cookie cutters spell G - O - O - D

Gingersnaps, Initially Yours

For corporate team building events, I spell out the company name with these cookies for dessert

- 3/4 cup unsalted butter — softened, (1 1/2 sticks)
- 1 cup honey — (12 oz. bottle)
- 2 eggs
- 1 teaspoon baking powder
- 1 Tablespoon ground ginger
- 1 Tablespoon ground cinnamon
- 1 teaspoon ground cloves
- 5 cups all-purpose flour

1. In large bowl, cream honey and butter until light and fluffy. Beat in eggs.
2. Stir in baking powder, ginger, cinnamon and cloves. Add flour and mix until combined. Wrap dough in plastic wrap and refrigerate for at least 2 hours.
3. When dough is chilled, divide dough in thirds; return remaining portions to refrigerator. Dust work surface and dough with flour. Roll out dough to 1/4-inch thick. Cut into desired shapes using cookie cutters. Transfer to baking sheet prepared with parchment paper. Repeat with remaining dough.
4. Bake in a pre-heated 350F oven for 10–12 minutes. Remove cookies from baking sheet and cool on a wire rack.

Makes 36 servings.
Per Serving: 131 Calories; 4g Fat (29.1% calories from fat); 2g Protein; 21g Carbohydrate; 1g Dietary Fiber; 22mg Cholesterol; 19mg Sodium.

Pralines have many variations.
Melted marshmallows make this one my favorite.

Sweet Georgia Browns

2	cups pecan halves — (or pieces)
1	cup evaporated milk
2	cups light brown sugar
1/4	cup unsalted butter — (1/2 stick)
12	large marshmallows — cut in fourths
1	teaspoon cinnamon
1/4	teaspoon nutmeg

1. Toast pecans in a dry skillet, stirring continuously. When oil streaks are released from the pecans, transfer them to a bowl.
2. Mix milk, sugar and butter in a 2 quart saucepan. Over medium heat, bring mixture to just above the hard ball stage (270F on a candy thermometer) and remove from heat.
3. Quickly stir in the marshmallows to melt. Add the cinnamon and nutmeg, then fold in the pecans.
4. Drop by spoonfuls onto a pan prepared with foil or wax paper. Allow to cool for about an hour. Store in an airtight container, or wrap individually in plastic wrap.

Makes 24 servings.
Per Serving: 148 Calories; 9g Fat (51.1% calories from fat); 1g Protein; 17g Carbohydrate; 1g Dietary Fiber; 8mg Cholesterol; 18mg Sodium.

Blackberry preserves are tasty in this recipe, too.

Italian Crescent Crostata

2	cans crescent rolls
1 1/2	cups red raspberry preserves
3/4	cup pecans – or walnuts
1/2	cup raisins – or currants
1	egg – beaten
1/4	cup powdered sugar

1. Preheat oven to 350F.
2. Place 10 triangles in an ungreased 13 inch x 9 inch dish. Press together over the bottom of the dish and 1/2 inch up each side to form a crust.
3. Partially bake the crust for 10–12 minutes until light golden brown.
4. In a medium bowl, combine preserves, nuts and raisins. Spread over the crust.
5. Press together the remaining dough with fingertips and cut in strips. Create a lattice design over the preserve mixture. Brush with beaten egg.
6. Bake an additional 17–20 minutes until golden brown. Cool. Dust with powdered sugar.

The definitive recipe for any Italian dish has not yet appeared. We're still creating.

— Luigi Barzini

Makes 12 servings.
Per Serving: 194 Calories; 6g Fat (22.5% calories from fat); 2g Protein; 36g Carbohydrate; 1g Dietary Fiber; 18mg Cholesterol; 59mg Sodium.

My personal favorite of all French desserts.

Baked Ile Flottante

1	Tablespoon butter
3	egg whites
1/3	cup sugar
1/4	teaspoon vanilla
1/4	teaspoon almond extract
1/4	cup sliced almonds

1. Preheat oven to 350F. Lightly butter a 4 cup ceramic or glass dish. Prepare a bain-marie. (Literally translated, this is a water bath.) This is a combination of a dish larger than the original, which can be half filled with water to cook in the oven.
2. In a clean, grease free bowl, beat egg whites to soft peaks in an electric mixer.
3. Add sugar, vanilla, and almond extract to the egg whites, and continue to beat for about 1 minute. Turn off the mixer and gently fold in the sliced almonds.
4. Scoop and gently spread mixture into the buttered dish. Set dish gently in the bain-marie, and place in the oven for 20 minutes. Carefully remove from the oven. Be careful not to splash the hot water bath. Lift dish from the bath and allow to cool for at least 10 minutes.
5. Using a hot serrated knife, slice the ile flottante and place in a pool of crème anglaise. Alternately, pour the crème anglaise onto a large rimmed platter, and gently remove the ile flottante from the dish and place in the center. For a beautiful presentation, sprinkle a few sliced almonds around the island in the cream.

Makes 8 servings.
Per Serving: 78 Calories; 4g Fat (42.6% calories from fat); 2g Protein; 9g Carbohydrate; trace Dietary Fiber; 4mg Cholesterol; 36mg Sodium.

Start an evening atop La Tour Eiffel with a glass of champagne toasting the sunset, and then finish with this dessert … a night in Paris couldn't be better.

Classic Ile Flottante [The Floating Island] is prepared over a simmering mixture of equal parts milk and water. Spoon out eight portions, and poach for about 2 minutes on the first side, and one minute on the other. Remove immediately, and serve over the crème anglais as described above. Warning: If it begins to smell more like a latte, the milk is too hot, and will just melt your egg whites. Keep it to a slow, barely bubbling simmer for your best success. To make it interesting, try adding 1/4 teaspoon of an extract flavoring for each 1 1/2 cups of liquid.

Classic Crème Anglaise

1 cup milk
3 Tablespoons sugar
3 egg yolks – beaten

1. Combine milk and sugar in a heavy saucepan. Mix thoroughly. Bring to a gentle boil.
2. In a bowl, whisk the beaten yolks while slowly adding the hot milk mixture. Add back to the saucepan and heat gently until the crème coats the back of a spoon.
3. Refrigerate until ready for use.

Many desserts benefit from the addition of a little crème, n'est-ce pas?

The first trip you take to Paris is filled with wonder and excitement. The question is how will that trip affect the rest of your life? Like life, appreciating Paris is an evolutionary process fraught with oxymoron, hedonism, incredulity, unabashed joy, and ultimately love. Like life, there is an ineffable pleasure in the knowledge that you will be returning to a city that is at once both old and new, open both to revisiting and discovery. Maybe life is a metaphor for Paris.

— From a web travelogue

Makes 10 servings.
Per Serving: 47 Calories; 2g Fat (44.5% calories from fat); 2g Protein; 5g Carbohydrate; 0g Dietary Fiber; 67mg Cholesterol; 14mg Sodium.

Many sweet desserts have been served in these shells.

Fresh summer-ripe berries are a traditional filling.

Masterpiece Meringue Shell

3	egg whites
1/4	teaspoon cream of tartar
2/3	cup sugar

1. Heat oven to 275F. Cut parchment paper to line baking sheet. Draw one 9-inch circle or 8 3-inch circles for a pattern on the bottom side of the paper. Wipe the cookie sheet with a moist sponge to adhere parchment. Set aside.
2. In a mixer, beat egg whites and cream of tartar on high speed until mixture begins to foam. Gradually add sugar until stiff and glossy. Shape on the cookie sheet pattern, building up the sides to hold filling.

3a. (Large) Bake 1 1/2 hours. Turn off the oven and let meringue cool slowly in the oven (door closed!) for one hour.

3b. (Individual) Bake one hour. Turn off the oven and let meringue cool slowly in the oven (door closed!) for one hour.

The kitchen is a country in which there are always discoveries to be made.

— Grimod de la Reynière (1758–1837)
author of ***L'Almanach des gourmands***

Makes 8 servings.
Per Serving: 71 Calories; 0g Fat (0.0% calories from fat); 1g Protein; 17g Carbohydrate; 0g Dietary Fiber; 0mg Cholesterol; 21mg Sodium.

Margarita Delight

Masterpiece Meringue Shell(s)
3/4 cup margarita mix – bottled
3 Tablespoons cornstarch
3/4 cup sugar
1/2 teaspoon salt
3 egg yolks – beaten
1 Tablespoon unsalted butter
1/3 cup lemon juice
1 lime – juiced
1 Tablespoon lime zest
2 Tablespoons sugar – tinted green

Sorority party inspired.
Forkfuls of goodness proven!
Delta Phi Nu

1. Prepare and cool a large meringue shell, or individual shells.
2. Blend 1/4 cup margarita mix with cornstarch and set aside. Mix sugar, remaining margarita mix, and salt in a 2-quart saucepan. Heat to a gentle boil. Add cornstarch mixture to saucepan, stirring constantly and bring to a boil. Boil for about two minutes to thicken.
3. Remove about 1/2 cup of the hot liquid, and gradually stir in to the egg yolks. Pour back into the saucepan, stirring constantly, and bring to a boil. Boil for about a minute to thicken and remove from heat.
4. Immediately add butter and stir to incorporate. Add lemon and lime juice to the mixture and cool to room temperature.
5. Spoon into the meringue shell, and refrigerate for at least 12 hours. Create a margarita rim of the sugar and lime zest around the edge of the shell, and serve.

Makes 8 servings.
Per Serving (without Meringue Shell): 155 Calories;
3g Fat (19.1% calories from fat); 1g Protein; 31g Carbohydrate;
trace Dietary Fiber; 84mg Cholesterol; 152mg Sodium.

Gelato Ravioli with Strawberry Purée

- 1 pie crust box – refrigerated; folded or rolled
- 1 pint fresh strawberries – (reserve 9)
- 2 Tablespoons Grand Marnier
- 2 Tablespoons granulated sugar
- 1 pint vanilla gelato
- 1/4 cup creme fraiche
- mint leaves

You can cut each pie pastry into 16 pieces and use with mini-muffin tins for multiple small desserts.

1. Preheat oven to 350F. Trim pie crusts into two 8 inch squares. Cut each crust into nine 2 1/2 inch squares.
2. Using an inverted muffin tin, drape 9 regular tins with the pastry, cupping them slightly. Place the other 9 squares on a baking sheet. Bake for 5–8 minutes until light brown. Let cool.
3. Reserve 9 pretty strawberries for garnish. De-stem remaining strawberries and puree in small food processor with Grand Marnier and sugar. Chill.
4. When ready to serve, spoon up to 1/4 cup of strawberry sauce on the plate. Place flat pastry in the center of the plate. Place small scoop of gelato on the pastry and cover with ravioli cup.
5. Spoon creme fraiche on top or the side. Add mint leaf and reserved strawberry.

With 9 servings, there is one left for the host after the guests depart. Hide it well.

Makes 9 servings.
Per Serving: 245 Calories; 13g Fat (49.4% calories from fat); 3g Protein; 26g Carbohydrate; 1g Dietary Fiber; 28mg Cholesterol; 168mg Sodium.

Apricot Double Chocolate Truffles

Choose your chocolate types carefully. The semi-sweet chips combined with baking chocolate gives a dark chocolate flavor. The milk chocolate gives a smooth taste, but it takes longer to become firm in the freezer. Mixing types of baking chocolate, chocolate bars and chips is encouraged in your own experiments.

6 ounces dried apricots – cut in 1/2 inch pieces
1 Tablespoon Brandy
1 Tablespoon water
1/2 cup whipping cream
1 cup baking chocolate squares – 8 ounces
1 cup semi-sweet chocolate chips
1/4 cup unsalted butter
2 Tablespoons shortening
1 cup milk chocolate chips – (or semi-sweet)
1/2 cup nuts – finely chopped
1/4 cup powdered sugar
1/2 teaspoon milk

1. Place apricots in a glass dish with the brandy and water. Cover with plastic wrap, and microwave for 30 seconds. Allow to sit while preparing other ingredients.
2. Mix cream, 2 cups chocolate and butter in the top of a double boiler. Mix until well melted. Add apricots and cover them in chocolate. Remove with a spoon to a lined cookie sheet. Cover with wax paper and set in freezer for 15 minutes, or until firm.
3. Mix shortening and 1 cup chocolate in the top of the double boiler. Mix until well melted. Remove from heat. Working quickly, roll each truffle in the melted chocolate, then roll in nuts. Return the truffles to the cookie sheet. Alternately, you can dip the truffle, and then drizzle with the powdered sugar and milk mixture.
4. When all truffles are complete, return to freezer for 30 minutes or until firm. Store in airtight containers.

"Sharing food with another human being is an intimate act that should not be indulged in lightly."

— M.F.K. Fisher, U.S. Culinary Expert

Makes 36 servings.
Per Serving: 122 Calories; 9g Fat (62.4% calories from fat); 1g Protein; 11g Carbohydrate; 2g Dietary Fiber; 9mg Cholesterol; 7mg Sodium.

Surprisingly low in fat, and genuinely moist without icing.

Gâteau Carotte D'Oliveira

For the days when mon ami George "takes the cake"

- 2 cups shredded carrots
- 1 cup all-purpose flour
- 1 cup wheat flour
- 1 cup sugar
- 2 teaspoons cinnamon
- 2 teaspoons baking soda
- 1/2 teaspoon ginger
- 1/2 teaspoon nutmeg
- 1/2 teaspoon cloves
- 1/2 teaspoon salt
- 1/2 cup applesauce, unsweetened
- 8 ounces lowfat yogurt
- 8 ounces crushed pineapple – reserve juice
- 1/4 cup vegetable oil
- 2 eggs
- 1 Tablespoon maple syrup
- 2 teaspoons vanilla

1. Preheat oven to 350F. Prepare a 9 inch x 13 inch pan with a non-stick spray.
2. In a large bowl, mix together carrots, flours, sugar, cinnamon, soda, ginger, nutmeg, cloves and salt with a fork until well combined.
3. Add remaining ingredients. Using an electric mixer, combine until smooth.
4. Pour into baking dish and place in oven for 45 minutes. Rotate cake in the oven after 20 minutes. Cake will spring to the touch in the center when ready.

If desired, make a sauce for ice cream served alongside cake. Heat the reserved pineapple juice, 2 tablespoons sugar and 1 Tablespoon orange zest in a small saucepan until slightly boiling and sugar is well dissolved. Cool. Drizzle over vanilla ice cream and place additional orange zest on top.

Makes 12 servings.
Per Serving: 232 Calories; 6g Fat (22.1% calories from fat); 5g Protein; 41g Carbohydrate; 3g Dietary Fiber; 36mg Cholesterol; 334mg Sodium.

These cut-out cookies serve many holiday and fun occasions

Windowpane Cookies

1/2 cup shortening – butter flavor
3 Tablespoons unsalted butter
1 cup sugar
2 eggs – lightly beaten
1/2 teaspoon vanilla extract
1/4 teaspoon almond extract
3 cups all-purpose flour
2 teaspoons baking powder
1/2 teaspoon salt
1/3 cup lowfat 1% milk
1/2 cup butterscotch candy – (about 20 pieces)
1/2 cup cinnamon candy – (about 20 pieces)

1. Preheat oven to 350F. Prepare cookie sheets with parchment paper.
2. In a large bowl, cream together the shortening, butter and sugar with a hand mixer. Add the eggs and extracts. In another bowl, lightly toss together the flour, baking powder and salt with a fork.
3. Blend about half the flour mixture with the egg mixture. Pour in milk and stir. Then add remaining flour mixture and mix well. [NOTE: If you are adding food coloring, it is best to separate the dough and add it now.]
4. Using a spatula, place dough in the center of a 13 inch x 9 inch piece of plastic wrap. Roll the dough to a 1 1/2 inch diameter. Refrigerate for at least an hour, however, its best with two.
5. Using different plastic bags for each color, put candies in bags and cover with dishcloth before crushing with a meat mallet.
6. When the dough is ready, remove from wrap onto a lightly floured surface. Making a less than 1/2 inch slice, place cookie dough on parchment. Using an apple corer or other small cookie cutter, remove a shape from the interior of the cookie. Taking the crushed candy, fill the window.
7. Bake for 10 minutes and turn in the oven. Bake for 2–5 minutes more until lightly browned on the edges. Remove pans to a cooling rack. ***Important!*** Leave cookies on baking sheet for 5–6 minutes, until the candy turns hard. Gently remove from the parchment with a spatula to a plate.

Makes 30 servings.
Per Serving: 129 Calories; 5g Fat (35.6% calories from fat); 2g Protein; 19g Carbohydrate; trace Dietary Fiber; 18mg Cholesterol; 85mg Sodium.

Shapes can include:

- *Center cut out of a heart, filled with red candy only.*
- *Two small rounds joined together with a black licorice stick for a butterfly. Cut two circles in each wing and vary the candy colors.*
- *Color most of the dough orange for a pumpkin with yellow eyes and a green dough stem.*
- *Dust a skull shape with powdered sugar and use red candies for the eyes and mouth.*

What now?
Candy melt too much? Sprinkle a bit more of the candy in the cut out as soon as it comes out of the oven. It will melt while it sits the few minutes on the baking sheet.

Miel Madeleines

4 eggs – plus 1 yolk
3/4 cup unsalted butter – softened
1/4 cup honey
1 Tablespoon lemon zest
3/4 cup sugar
1/4 cup brown sugar, packed – (or 3 Tablespoons raw sugar)
1/2 teaspoon vanilla
1/2 teaspoon almond extract
1 cup almonds – ground fine
1 cup all-purpose flour
1 teaspoon baking powder
1/4 teaspoon salt
powdered sugar

1. Preheat oven to 375F.
2. Place the whole, unbroken eggs in a large mixing bowl filled with hot tap water. Grease the madeleine pan using shortening, or use a non-stick cooking spray.
3. Warm the butter pieces in a small dish until they are partially melted. Remove from the heat and stir until completely melted; the butter should be the consistency of light cream. Add honey to the warmed butter and stir in the lemon zest. Set the butter mixture aside. When you are ready to use the butter, it should be the consistency of heavy cream.

The time in the freezer is critical for even baking and reducing the risk of burned edges.

*What now?
No Madeleine pan?
A mini-muffin tin will hold these and increase your cooking time no more than five minutes.*

An invitation to New Year's Day lunch out in the country is a welcome start for a new year. After driving about an hour and a half out of Paris, we find clean, crisp air with just a trace of rain. As I looked across the moist plains of grass, I felt a silent word of welcome from the landscape.

— ChefKAT's Adventures in Paris, 2003

4. Remove the eggs from the bowl and pour out the water. In the same warm bowl, beat the eggs and yolk on high. Add the sugars and extracts to the mixture, and continue on high until it triples in volume, about 5–8 minutes. The batter should be very thick. It will fall slowly from the beaters and stand on the surface.
5. In a small bowl, thoroughly combine the ground almond mixture, flour, baking powder and salt. Sprinkle the flour mixture one-third at a time onto the surface of the batter. Using a rubber spatula, fold the flour in gently. Fold no more than 10-12 times per addition. After the last addition, there may be a small amount of flour visible.
6. Fold approximately 1 cup of the batter into the creamy butter combination until well blended. Pour this mixture into the remaining batter and fold gently no more than 10–12 times. The batter will begin to fall with streaks of butter. A completely smooth batter is not necessary.
7. Spoon the fluffy mixture into the madeleine pans, and wipe any excess from the cup edges. Place the filled pan into the freezer for at least 30 minutes, and no more than two hours. The will cause the thin edges of the dough to firm up and almost freeze.
8. When ready, place the pans into the oven and lower the temperature to 350F. Watching carefully, check the madeleines at 8 minutes, and bake no longer than 15 minutes. The tops should be firm to the touch, and spring back when gently pressed. Turn out onto a cooling rack to show the classic baked pattern. Sprinkle lightly with powdered sugar and serve.

Makes 24 servings.
Per Serving: 161 Calories; 10g Fat (52.7% calories from fat); 3g Protein; 17g Carbohydrate; 1g Dietary Fiber; 51mg Cholesterol; 57mg Sodium.

Individual Orange Baked Alaskas

- 8 oranges
- 1 quart vanilla ice cream – barely softened
- 2 egg whites – room temperature
- 6 tablespoons sugar
- 1/4 teaspoon cream of tartar
- 1 teaspoon vanilla

1. Slice the top off each orange and scoop out the pulp. Set orange shells on a cookie sheet. Fill each shell with a scoop of ice cream. Place shells in freezer to firm.
2. Beat egg whites until stiff but not dry. Gradually beat in sugar and cream of tartar. Continue beating until very smooth and glossy. Add vanilla.
3. Remove shells from freezer and smooth meringue over the ice cream filled orange shells. Re-freeze.
4. Just before serving, preheat broiler. Bake Alaskas just until meringue on top is lightly browned, about 3 to 5 minutes.

Easily prepared; impressive dessert

Sugar was regarded as a spice and was imported from all over the Mediterranean. It was a costly ingredient, available only to the wealthier members of society with sugar loaves being a welcome gift. There was much symbolism and significance in the great state banquets. Sugar sculptures, known as subtleties, were often produced to convey political or social messages.

— The Great Kitchens of Stirling Castle

Makes 8 servings.
Per Serving: 236 Calories; 7g Fat (27.0% calories from fat); 4g Protein; 41g Carbohydrate; 3g Dietary Fiber; 29mg Cholesterol; 67mg Sodium.

Hawaiian Alohas

1 1/2	cups macadamia nuts – toasted
1	cup granulated sugar
1	cup light brown sugar
2	Tablespoons unsalted butter
1 1/2	cups heavy cream
1	teaspoon light corn syrup
1/2	cup white chocolate – (4–5 ounces) chopped

Try serving these on a tray surrounded by a flower lei.

1. Toast the macadamia nuts in a small dry skillet. Stir continuously to prevent scorching. When the scent of macadamia starts to waft from the pan, remove from heat to a small bowl.
2. Mix together the sugars, butter, cream and corn syrup in a 2 quart saucepan. Heat to firm-ball stage. (245F on a candy thermometer)
3. Quickly stir the chocolate into the sugar mixture until melted. Add toasted nuts.
4. Drop by spoonfuls onto a pan prepared with foil or wax paper. Allow to cool for about 15 minutes. Remove to an airtight container, or wrap individually in plastic wrap.

Makes 24 servings.
Per Serving: 199 Calories; 14g Fat (61.6% calories from fat); 1g Protein; 19g Carbohydrate; 1g Dietary Fiber; 23mg Cholesterol; 10mg Sodium.

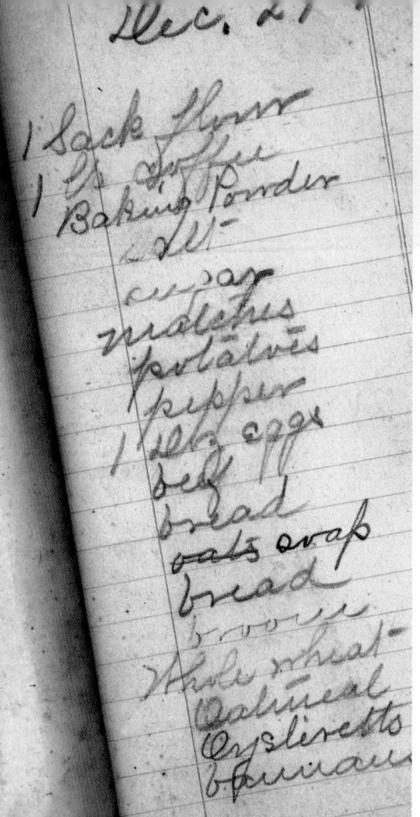

How to stock a new kitchen with the basics

Baking Products:

White all-purpose flour
Whole wheat flour (optional)
Bread crumbs (optional)
Corn meal
Shortening (optional)
Bread crumbs (optional)
Oil (Vegetable &/or Olive)
Baking soda
Vanilla
Granulated sugar
Brown sugar
Sugar substitute (optional)
Biscuit mix (optional)
Cornstarch (optional)
Yeast
Non-stick spray
Baking powder
Powdered sugar (optional)
Salt
Pepper

Dried Spices:

* Basil
* Bay leaves
Chili powder
* Cinnamon
Cayenne pepper
Curry powder
Fruit Fresh®
Garlic powder
Nutmeg
* Oregano
Paprika
* Rosemary
Red pepper flakes
Tabasco®
* Thyme

* The standard six

Jar/Canned Fruits & Vegetables:

Peaches &/or Pears
Pineapple
Green beans
Red kidney beans
Tomatoes
Tomato sauce/Spaghetti sauce

Pasta:

Rice
Penne &/or Rotini
Spaghetti

Frozen Goods:

Whole ear corn or kernels
Broccoli or spinach
Peas
Pie shell or folded crusts
Waffles
Orange juice
Cool Whip®
Pizza

Condiments:

Mayonnaise
Mustard
Ketchup
Salad dressing
Salad vinegar
Salsa
Steak sauce/Worcestershire/BBQ sauce
Soy sauce

Dairy products:

Milk
Buttermilk (optional)
Butter/Margarine
Eggs
Sour cream
Plain yogurt (optional)
Cheese (cheddar & mozzarella)
Parmesan cheese

On the Bookshelf:

Betty Crocker Cookbook
or
The Joy of Cooking

New Basics Cookbook
by Rosso & Lukins

Ethnic cookbook of choice

Breads/Cereals:

- Bread
- Bagels or English muffins
- Oatmeal (Quick/Old-Fashioned)
- Flour tortillas
- Corn flakes (plain cereal)
- Golden Grahams® (sweet cereal)

Miscellaneous:

- Peanut butter
- Tuna
- Jam/Jelly/Preserves
- Pancake syrup
- Chicken/Beef bouillon
- Coffee/Tea
- Popcorn or pretzels
- Crackers or chips
- Cookies
- Pudding mix
- Soft drinks

Pots/Pans/Bakeware:

- 2 cup saucepan with lid
- 2–3-quart saucepan with lid
- 10"–12" Sauté/Fry pan with lid
- Dutch oven
- Roasting pan
- Pasta pot (optional)
- 2-quart ovenproof casserole
- 6-quart ovenproof casserole
- 13" x 9" baking dish
- 8" x 8" baking dish (optional)
- 2 cookie sheets
- Muffin tin
- 2 round cake pans (8" or 9")
- Glass pie plate

Electrical Equipment:

- Hand-mixer or stand-up mixer
- Blender
- Toaster
- Food processor (optional)

Knives:

- 10" Chef's knife
- 6"–8" Slicing knife
- Paring knife
- Serrated knife
- Cutting boards (large and small)

Utensils:

- 4 graduated mixing bowls (2 cup to 3 quart)
- Measuring spoons
- Glass measuring cup (1 cup and larger)
- Dry measuring cup set
- Long handled spoon (stainless &/or for non-stick)
- Long handled slotted spoon (stainless &/or for non-stick)
- Long handled wooden spoons
- Long handled fork
- Rubber spatula
- Heat resistant spatula (optional)
- Long handled large metal spatula
- Kitchen tongs
- Rolling pin
- Soup ladle
- 8" stainless steel wire whisk
- Grater
- 2 wire mesh strainers (3" & 7" round)
- Colander
- Funnel
- Potholders
- Bottle opener
- Can opener
- Instant read thermometer
- Garlic press
- Vegetable peeler
- Corkscrew
- Pepper grinder
- Kitchen timer
- Apple slicer/corer (optional)
- Microplane® (optional)

Bibliography

Brand, Joshua, and John Falsey. *Chris in the Morning: Love Life and the Whole Karmic Enchilada.* Chicago, Contemporary Books, 1993.

Bond, Marybeth. *Gutsy Women: more travel tips and wisdom for the road.* San Francisco, Travelers' Tales, 2001.

Edelman, Marian Wright. *Roar Softly and Carry a Great Lipstick: 28 Women Writers on Life, Sex, and Survival.* Maui, Autumn Stephens, 2004.

Gallimore, Byron and Hill, Faith. *This Kiss.* Album Faith. Puckalesia Song/Nomad-Noman Music/Warner-Tamerlane Publishing Corp. Warner Bros, 1998.

Hemingway, Ernest. *Christmas on the Roof of the World.* Toronto, Toronto Star Syndicated, 1923.

Hoff, Benjamin. *The Tao of Pooh.* New York, Penguin Group, 1982.

Sendak, Maurice. *Where the Wild Things Are.* New York, Harper Collins, 1963.

Silverstein, Shel. *Where the Sidewalk Ends.* New York, Harper Collins, 1974.

Theophano, Janet. *Eat My Words: Reading Women's Lives through the Cookbooks They Wrote.* New York: Palgrave, 2002.

Thorne, John. *Perfect Food.* New York, Simple Cooking, 1996.

WineGardner, Mark. *We Are What We Ate.* Orlando, Share our Strength, 1998.

Index